1

The Disciplined Mind

Strengthen Your Willpower, Develop Mental
Toughness, Control Your Thoughts, and Get
Rid of Your Inner Critic

By Zoe McKey

Communication Coach and

Social Development Trainer

zoemckey@gmail.com

www.zoemckey.com

Thank you for choosing my book! I would like to show my appreciation for the trust you gave me by giving **FREE GIFTS** for you!

For more information visit www.zoemckey.com

The checklist talks about *5 key elements of building self-confidence* and contains extra actionable worksheets with practice exercises for deeper learning.

Learn how to:

- Solve 80% of you self-esteem issues with one simple change
- Keep your confidence permanent without falling back to self-doubt
- Not fall into the trap of promising words
- Overcome anxiety
- Be confident among other people

The cheat sheet teaches you three key daily routine techniques to become more productive, have less stress in your life, and be more well-balanced. It also has a step-by-step sample sheet that you can fill in with your daily routines.

Discover how to:

- Overcome procrastination following 8 simple steps
- Become more organized
- Design your yearly, monthly, weekly and daily tasks in the most productive way.
- 3 easy tricks to level up your mornings

professional person should be sought. The author shall not be liable for damages arising herefrom. The fact that an individual, organization of website is referred to in this work as a citation and/or potential source of further information does not mean that the author endorses the information the individual, organization to website may provide or recommendations they/it may make. Further, readers should be aware that Internet websites listed in this work might have changed or disappeared between when this work was written and when it is read.

For general information on the products and services or to obtain technical support, please contact the author.

Table of Contents

Introduction

Once upon a time, my life took a switch. I moved away from home, Romania, to pursue better opportunities in Hungary where I earned a scholarship. My parents weren't exactly made of money. Unable to afford renting an apartment, I was placed in the high school's free dorm. The free dorm offered exactly what one would think: a place where I could keep my stuff, sleep, and clean myself. Nothing more. Before you start brainstorming what else I would need, I'll give you a hint: food. Surprisingly, food was not included. "At least I can bathe before I die of hunger," I thought dramatically with my fourteen-year-old brain.

It was not the school's problem that I couldn't afford the cheap canteen meals in the dorm's kitchen, which were designed to feed poor kids like me. I was even poorer than the rest. But I had a strong sense of pride and kept my head held high, defiantly refusing to ask for help. I looked at it as: I'm a big girl, I'll deal with it.

I "dealt with the problem" by sulking in the kitchen at lunchtime, watching the others eat, hoping that someone would give me his or her lunch. That never happened. The best I could hope for was that someone would leave an unfinished meal on the table so I could feast upon the rest. Even then, my foolish pride kept me fasting instead of feasting, as I was worried someone else would see me. I was a typical self-conscious teenager concerned with my image. I would reason, "No, I'm not hungry. I already ate this week." So I just sat, sulked, and prayed the canteen lady didn't clean up the leftovers before I could.

I spent three days hoping that if I stayed around there long enough, I would get some food eventually. But I didn't. The only thing I heard besides my growling stomach was the canteen lady's sharp, loud voice. She always complained about how many dishes she had to collect and wash.

Aha—a light bulb moment!

The next day, after lunchtime was over, I went down to the kitchen and started collecting the dishes, carrying them to the dish collector cart. The canteen lady was very surprised and grateful for my help. My stomach, like a well-trained dog, started growling loudly at just the right moment, sending a clear message to the mother of three. The canteen lady told me there were lots of leftovers, so if I was hungry, she could give me a plate or two. Or, as many as I wanted, really, because otherwise, she would just throw the food away. From that moment on, I had a job and a salary, bartering my work for food.

Going back to the quote at the beginning of the chapter, I realized I couldn't change the schooling system in Hungary. I couldn't make the Ministry of Education include free meals along with free tuition and housing. Even if I succeeded, it would have been too late to improve my situation. The solution to my problem was right in front of me, and luckily, I took the opportunity to change what I could. The impact was great and immediate.

The things you can't change are those things you can't control.

Consequently, the things you can change are those that fall under your control. Today, people want to feel in control, and when they're not, they become desperate. In this state of desperation, they overlook some solutions that could also solve their problems. In my case, I wanted to change the system, the minds of my classmates, basically everything else before I thought about changing my attitude.

I rephrased Niebuhr's saying: Grant me the serenity to accept the things I *cannot control,* courage to change the things I *can control*, and wisdom to know the difference.

One thing that you can control is your time. Not time in general. You can't make twenty-six hour days but you can control what you do in the twenty-four you have. Many of your control-related frustrations are rooted in bad time management. Let's take as an example a situation when you stand in a long line in the supermarket.

Situation A: You woke up on time, knowing you needed to drop by and pick up some breakfast before work, so you calculated how much time that would take as a worst-case scenario and left your house just in time. While you waited in the line, you read the news, checked your social media, read a book, or double-checked your presentation so you didn't have dead time while you waited. When you finally got to the checkout, you paid and headed to work.

Situation B: You had a delay. You knew you should have woken up earlier, but the bed was so inviting that you indulged yourself and slept five minutes more. And five more minutes, again and again... Thirty minutes after the first alarm, you jumped out of bed in a hurry, did a perfunctory job with your hair and dress, and rushed to your car to get to the supermarket to grab some food. You hit a long line even though you collected what you wanted in thirty seconds. You looked at your watch five times per minute, impatiently tapping your leg. All you could hear in your mind was, "I'm going to be late. I'm going to be so late. My boss will scold me, I'll get angry and won't be able to finish my job. Life is so unfair! Why does this line have to be so long? Unbelievable! Why do bad things always have to happen to me? I must have done something very bad in a previous life. Come on, hurry up!"

The same situation, different time-management. What was the difference between the two examples? The method of how you took advantage of time. In the first example, you prepared yourself for unforeseeable hindrances, things you couldn't control, added them to you time-management plans, and executed your morning plans accordingly. You made uncontrollable events controllable by managing your time well. With self-control and good time management, you could handle even the uncontrollable things. Things beyond your control still happened, but you didn't let it affect your plans.

In situation B, you didn't have any kind of control. You had no self-control when you had to wake up. You didn't make any time management plans that would allow you to adapt to uncontrollable situations. You didn't have the flexibility to change your plans knowing you were faced with a delay. Stubbornly, without any sense of responsibility, you followed your plans. You hoped no one would be in the line when you went to the supermarket even though you knew that there is a morning rush there every day.

On the way to the supermarket, you made up different explanations in your mind why people would not be in front of you. When things turned out differently, you started panicking and rationalizing why everything and everybody but you were at fault for the delay you were in. Every spirit aligned against you, pulling Mars to close a twenty-degree angle with Jupiter just for the sole purpose of making you late. You already decided that your boss would be angry and you'd have a bad day.

Who behaves like the person in situation B? Someone with no self-control, no sense of responsibility, and lacking priorities.

We are not machines. We get in situation Bs more often than we'd like to; sometimes even when we take possible unexpected events into consideration and try to keep our time under control. Regardless of the reasons, let's see how we can better handle the situation Bs in life.

The most important step is to take total responsibility for your actions. Regardless of whether you are at fault for your problems (like oversleeping) or not (an accident ahead of you on the highway), the responsibility is still yours to take.

Do not mistake the words culpable and responsible, they are not synonyms. People often don't take responsibility because they think it will make them *culpable* as well. When you are not at fault, if something goes wrong in your life, it's still your responsibility to make it right.

For example, if you leave for work in plenty of time but there is an accident on the highway that causes you to be stuck in traffic for hours. It's not your fault the accident happened, but it is your responsibility to call your workplace and tell your boss that you're going to be late.

You may not be at fault, but at the end of the day, you'll still be late to work.

There are times when you are at fault for something, you need to take responsibility for what was an involuntary mistake.

For example, you accidentally pour coffee on someone. It's your fault and you take responsibility for it, even though it was an accident. You didn't pour the coffee on the person on purpose (let's not imagine some bad soap opera scenario here, just a regular Monday rush), but the coffee is still on his shirt. Saying you're sorry and walking away won't make his shirt any less stained. You can offer to pay for the dry-cleaning. Most people won't accept money but they will feel less angry if you show true remorse and offer them a solution for the trouble you've caused.

Things occur in life where you're not culpable for what happened – and it' not something predictable, like a traffic jam on the highway often can be. For example, it turns out your baby will likely be born with a severe mental or physical illness. It's not your fault, but it is still your responsibility to make a decision, and you'll be responsible for the results of that decision. Whatever you choose, whether to keep the baby or have an abortion, there will be life-long consequences that you'll have to live with.

The more responsibility you take, the more control you'll have over your life. Why? As soon as you accept responsibility for something, you jump from the past to the present. Issues get solved in the present. As long as you stay in the past, you'll complain, try to find culprits, and victimize yourself. These "quasi-solutions" might give you peace of mind in the short term, but they won't solve your problem.

You can't control the length of the line at the supermarket, but how you react is your responsibility.   Do you get angry and frustrated? Stay in line against your better judgment? Decide to leave and order food later? Or do you call your boss to explain you'll be a bit late?

If you decided to stand in line and it resulted in you being late, own it and take responsibility for the consequences. It was not fate, a past life or the odds of shopping that conspired against you. It was just you, your bad time-management and lack of willpower to get up in time, or your refusal to walk away without food. Staying in line is a solution too. It won't help you with your boss, but it will give you a sense of being in control. Yes, you messed up, but you know you did it of your own free will and you're ready to accept the consequences.

Choose your priorities well. What are the steps you should think through to maximize your control and minimize hindrances in a situation?

1.   Know what you want to get out of the situation. What results do you need or want to achieve?

2. Identify any potential uncontrollable events that could delay or circumvent your plans.

3. Prepare preventative strategies to minimize the impact of any uncontrollable event as much as possible.

4. If the uncontrollable event happens, and it is worse than you expected, analyze what can you do to still meet your needs (established in point 1).

5.   Make a decision and take responsibility for it.

These guidelines can be applied to minor things, like the shopping misery mentioned above, as well as bigger problems. Taking responsibility as second nature requires training. Analyze your reactions to stressful situations and note which have affected your peace of mind the most.

Which are the life areas where you struggle to take responsibility? What situations make you the most defensive, angry, or discouraged?
Apply this five-point analysis to get through the event with a clearer mind, more control, and less stress.

Key takeaways to discipline your mind:

- The things you can change are those that fall under your control. Change them to best fit your life.

- Taking responsibility for your actions doesn't mean accepting culpability.

- Get clear with your most burning needs and wishes. Prioritize your actions in a way to make their completion unavoidable.

Chapter 1: Accept That Everything in Life is a Tradeoff

Mark Manson wrote a blog post based on a story he read on Facebook. I know, these two facts were already enough for you to question the depth of what I'm about to say, but hear me out, it will be worth it. [i]

This story was shared by CTV News, Canada. The main person involved was a man named Mohammed El-Erian, the CEO of a two trillion-dollar worth bond fund called PIMCO. Financially speaking, he was a wealthy man with a decent $100 million per year salary and an upward-running career.

Even though his career path was enviable and extraordinary, El-Erian decided to resign his position. Why would he do that, you might ask? What can be better than a $100 million salary? Maybe a $200 million one? Nope. Finding a better paying job was not his reason for quitting. He wanted to spend more time with his ten-year-old daughter.

Of course, news like this doesn't go unnoticed in our society. It circulated like wildfire because the reason behind his decision was somewhat contradictory to today's Western society values, namely to get rich, richer, the richest.

What on earth led El-Erian to this decision? The deal breaker day, when he came to his decision, began like any other day. He had an argument with his daughter about a trivial issue. He asked her to brush her teeth. When the little one refused, the dad, fueled by parental superiority and shortage of time and patience, supported his demand with the following argument: "I'm your father and you will do what I say." The little girl, hearing his reasoning, asked for her father's patience. She entered her room and a few minutes later came out with a paper, where she had written down twenty-two moments of her life in the current year where her father was not present because of his work.

These childishly scratched sentences of his daughter changed something in Mohammed El-Erian because the next day he quit his job despite his salary ridiculously rich in zeros. He chose to be a father for his child instead.

Economists call this phenomenon paying the "opportunity cost." I just call it the "something for something principle." In other words, anything you choose to do will cost you in not doing something else.

You can't have it all. Every time you make a decision, an abundance of parallel universe choices fly out the window. If you choose to have a shiny career, you pay for it with your time and energy. Being more present at home will result in less presence in your work place. Choosing the Nutella donut will result in not having the cinnamon donut, and so on.

If you want to have a smooth journey on this earth, you have to accept one thing: you can't have everything; at least not at the same time.

Every choice you make is also a sacrifice. In the case of El-Erian, the something was his job, which he gave up for another something (someone), his daughter.

Every choice has a price. The bolder the choice, the bigger "opportunity cost" you have to pay. Some people are admired in our society for their money and success. Yet, there is an equally huge opportunity cost behind them, and many things they gave up for their success. Bill Gates was famous for sleeping in his office, Angelina Jolie can't make a step without being photographed, or harassed by the media. Don't feel sorry for them. Their fate was their choice and they are responsible for it.

Every great achievement comes with great costs.

Everything one chooses to do removes him from another opportunity he could do instead. Therefore, when someone chooses to spend his time doing you a favor, he expects a reward for it. If you go to work for a company, you expect a salary. You trade your time for money. I collected the dishes for the canteen lady and expected food in return. Just as she expected me to do the dishes before giving me food. If someone helps you with your work, they expect something else in return: your goodwill or help, or your peanut butter muffins.

People hardly ever do anything unless there is something in it for them. I learned this lesson well in my hungry teenage years. When I just sat passively in the kitchen, I went to bed hungry. The canteen lady just washed her dishes and went home exhausted. Both of us were losers at the end of the day. The supply and demand sat face to face but for some reason they ignored each other. I didn't ask for food, and she didn't ask for help. When my hunger finally showed me the way, we left the kitchen with a win-win feeling. We both added something in the value basket and took something out of it.

How costly is opportunity anyway?

The world is much more complex than ancient barter. We have so many opportunities that alluringly invite us to choose them. The abundance of choice created by modern society makes the opportunity costs seem higher than ever before. To choose something, we perceive that we say no to ten things which increases our remorse and triggers our guilt.

People constantly feel insecure about their choices. "What if I wasted time by doing this? I could have done that instead. I would have been so much happier, more productive, etc."

The world isn't going easy on you, is it? In the age when the ancient barter was trending, everybody had their role in society. The role was determined by birth much of the time. Those who were born farmers didn't have another choice than being a farmer. The son of the blacksmith inherited the workshop and the profession from his father. The sick and weak son of the blacksmith became the next priest of the village. These people didn't aim for anything else other than becoming a good farmer or a talented blacksmith – partly because they weren't aware of anything else being available to them, and partly because they felt no pressure in "leveling-up their lives." They had it all in an old sense of the meaning. The farmer brought fresh products to the blacksmith who sharpened the gardening tools of the farmer in return. This was the rudimentary art of a deal.

Not today. Today there are so many opportunities, and what's more, we are reminded of these opportunities so often that regardless of the choices we make, we end up feeling regret and like we are missing something.

If you choose to be a successful business owner, you'll inevitably have to decrease time spent on your love life, or with your family, friends, and hobbies proportionately in order to prioritize your business. Books, movies, and advertisements will put the importance of family, love, and healthy hobbies on constant full display, triggering a sense of loss and regret in you.

If you choose to be a boring but useful piece of society, you'll look resentfully on the rich and beautiful. If you're living an extraordinary, glamorous life, you might wish to have a quiet little lodge somewhere near the Canadian border away from all the fame and fuss.

What is the solution to breaking out of the "fear of missing out" (FOMO) rut? More money? "Like it's that easy," you might say. You're right. It is not that easy. Having *enough* money is not purely under your control. You can't say, "I want a million dollars," and the next hour the guy from DLS knocks your door with a special delivery.

I've been reflecting a lot on how to answer the question of how to break the FOMO rut myself. My mind was very undisciplined and troubled about the choices I felt I had missed over the years. Then one day I came up with an answer.

As the previous chapter concluded, you can change only those things that are under your control. What is under your control in the case of the FOMO rut?

Your needs and wants.

You can't fully control your income – especially if you are a business owner. You certainly can't generate more time. Even in the span of your twenty-four hours you can't have total control. An unexpected accident on the highway, a broken oven, a power outage, and all your plans can go down the drain. Don't stress over things you can't change. Focus on what you can control instead – your own heart's desires.

Mark Manson contemplates, "What if the solution is simply accepting our bounded potential, our unfortunate tendency as humans to inhabit only one place in space and time? What if we recognize our life's inevitable limitations and then prioritize what we care about based on those limitations?"[ii]

People who complain about a tiring job, lack of time, being stuck in a rut, feeling that their lives are not heading anywhere, having no personal life, or that they don't know what to do to turn their lives around, usually have one single problem.

They don't know what their real priorities in life are.

Do you know what yours are? What is your most important goal in life? What goal are you willing to sacrifice the most for? There is no wrong answer to these questions. Crystalize what your most important goal is and focus your time and energy accordingly.

If you think that family and career is equally important to you, don't worry. There is a solution to have them both. You can't have everything. However, you can have something all the time. Look at El-Erian. First, he focused on his career, sacrificing everything for his career's sake. He persisted and made it. Then he gave up his career for everything else. Once he had the money, he could be truly present in his daughter's life without worrying about his financial life.

Now that you are aware of the "something for something principle" let's see how can you use it in everyday life.

In business, people will only help you if you can compensate them somehow for their time, effort, and knowledge. Nobody works for free. Just like you, they are also working hard to reach their goals.

How would you feel if someone asked for your help and then disappeared, taking advantage of you by stealing your time? Maybe you'd be pissed but you'd get over it, right? Okay, then let's change the word time for money; "taking advantage of you by stealing your money." I bet you'd be furious. Time is money one way or another. I'd say time is even more precious than money. Next time, before you ask someone for help, consider the following: what can I do for this person to get what I want?

What can I give to get?

Who would you rather help? Someone who comes to you asking for your peanuts or someone who offers you candies first for your peanuts?

Human nature is coded to equalize the balance between how much we give and get. In most cases, people focus on the get side of the equation because they don't want to give more than they get.

However, people also hate to feel indebted to others. Did a colleague ever treat you to coffee and you felt uncomfortable around them until you reciprocated? What's more, because your colleague offered his treat so selflessly the other day, you wanted to show some extra appreciation, more than just equalizing the balance, so you added a cookie to the coffee treat. Now your colleague feels indebted, so the next time he'll bring an extra muffin his wife just baked to give to you... And so on.

If we give first, we will start to get more.

One day I found a wallet full of money. The evil advisor inside me quickly sat on my left shoulder whispering, "Take the money and run! You won't have to wash dishes for weeks!"

"Yeah, you're right, evil little voice in my head. I hate dishwashing anyway. I will save so much time and eat much better food than leftovers."

However, another voice spoke up on my right shoulder. "Take a look at this old wallet. Someone worked hard for that money. How could you take that away? You have the possibility to eat. If you take the money, this person might not have that chance." Cursing my good side, I decided to take a look for an ID in the wallet, hoping to see a twenty-year-old yahoo who just lost his lunch money. Instead, I recognized a middle-aged man who held some classes quite often at my dorm's gym.

I went to the gym and saw that he was still there. I went to him and returned his wallet. He was very surprised to see me return his money. He had just finished his class, so we started talking. It turned out he was a three Dan Aikido master. While telling me stories about the Aikido philosophy, he noticed a glow of interest in my eyes. Unexpectedly, he asked me to try his classes.

For a moment I thought I misheard him. The very thought of belonging somewhere sounded more than inviting. I still felt like a stranger in the new city. I would have paid all the opportunity costs to do Aikido, but I knew I couldn't pay the financial costs. So I politely refused his offer. After a moment of consideration, he told me the money he had in his wallet would cover my membership fee for a year. If money was the reason why I declined his offer, I shouldn't worry because I just paid it.

I learned a great life lesson that day. What you give is what you get back. If you give good things to the world, you'll get good things back. Maybe your kindness won't be rewarded instantly. Maybe it won't be the same person who will repay it. But you'll get what you deserve eventually.

Don't forget. There's always an opportunity cost in your decisions. If you can help it, make sure you give first and give good things to others.

Key takeaways to discipline your mind:

- Accept that in life, everything is a payoff.
- You can have everything you want just not at the same time.
- Give before you expect to get something. This way you'll have the good will of others.

- Give more than you get. This way you'll get more than you expect.

Chapter 2: The Paradox of Responsibility

We live in the age of freedom. Freedom of speech, freedom of self-expression, and free Wi-Fi. I was born into it. You might have been born into it, too. Ultimately, we're the beneficiaries of a lot of advantages that have been earned through the sacrifice and blood of our ancestors.

Today we can access everything so easily, with so little sacrifice that we don't even consider the value, rather we tend to take things for granted. We feel entitled to these things even though we did nothing to earn them. Pleasures that are easily gained bring with them two main existential issues:

A: *People take everything for granted faster and easier.*

For example, there is a trial for free Wi-Fi on an airplane. Let's say someone messes something up and the internet access is lost after fifteen minutes. Following the mistake, a mini-riot breaks out on the plane, demanding internet connection. Wi-Fi on airplanes is uncommon, and hardly ever happens for free, or at all. Still, the passengers, after only fifteen minutes usage, got so used to the comfort of it that they viewed having free Wi-Fi as the new "normal." They felt entitled to their demand even if they never had internet connection on a plane before.

B: *People think they should get things without sacrifice.*

In the past fifty or sixty years, the standard of living radically improved almost everywhere in the world. Everything became more accessible, easier, and faster. Oddly enough, the happiness level didn't rise along with it. Psychologists have never been busier than they are today. The number of patients with mental illness, depression, and anxiety problems is through the roof.

As our feeling of self-importance grows, the importance the world places on the individual seemingly shrinks.

Why? On one hand, people's feelings of self-importance turns into narcissism, which prevents them from caring about the importance of others. On the other hand, the many distractions in the world make it impossible to be able to do everything one wants. Everybody is caught up in his or her own FOMO (fear of missing out). Caring about the issues others face probably won't be on their to-do list. And it shouldn't be expected.

Even if you build your hopes upon someone else solving your problems, they won't.

The world is not responsible for you. You're responsible for yourself in the world.

I experienced the paradox of responsibility early in my life, although it took me decades to act upon it. I still struggle occasionally with choosing to take responsibility instead of whining and blaming my problems on my unfortunate past and expecting the world to compensate me for them.

The first time I experienced the paradox of responsibility was right after I moved away from home. I was very young, lacking the knowledge needed to manage myself in a foreign country. I knew nothing about money management or state institutions and regulations. On top of my lack of knowledge, I was fourteen so nobody took me seriously. "Go and bring your parents, kid," officials told me.

One day, I received a notification from my school that I needed a document to confirm my permanent residence in the country. "Hey, I was playing with Barbie dolls a year ago! What is a permanent residence? What is a residence?" These were my first thoughts. However, I knew this problem wouldn't solve itself, so I went to ask for advice from the canteen lady. She told me to go to the immigration office and ask for information there.

When I went to the immigration office, I was told they couldn't issue a permanent residency paper unless the school confirmed that I legally studied there and lived in their dorm because of my studies. My school, however, wouldn't confirm my studies until I got the residency document. I was trapped in a bureaucratic catch

22. No one in the government office knew anything. They just sent me to another department, hoping to get rid of me. My school didn't know anything either except how to threaten to freeze my studies and my place in the dorm.

I thought the situation I was stuck in was completely unfair. My parents were far away, I had no one to care about my problems. Nobody seemed to care if I ended up on the streets and if I was denied my hard-earned scholarship. Why? Because of some bureaucratic loop the government was too lazy to develop properly. What could I do? First I cried, of course, and stressed, and fought with my parents, and then cried some more. Eventually I got tired of each of these unconstructive problem-solving options.

I had to take responsibility for my life. Nobody else would have done it. And why would they?

My problem was not their problem. Was I young? Sure I was, so what? Screaming it into the face of a clerk wouldn't have solved anything. "Bring your parents," they said. But my parents wouldn't come. They couldn't. They had no money and no idea how legislation worked in Hungary. I couldn't count on my dad coming in as my knight in shining armor to save me from the evil institutions. All I had was myself and my wish to stay where I was.

I clearly lacked the knowledge I needed to argue my case. What do you do when you lack knowledge? You research, study, and learn.

That's what I did. I went to the school's computer room and spent long hours every day after classes to search for the solution to my problem. It wasn't an easy ride – legal documents, immigration law, and exceptions... Come on! I had been building mud castles in my grandparents' yard that summer! Why did I have to deal with this three months later? Why? As much as I hoped, no answer came.

I was alone with my desperate mind. This is a tough and painful realization at any age but the quicker you accept it, the easier your life will be.

After a few days of research, I found an article that discussed imposing different treatments on foreign students and merging the terms of permanent residence and temporary residence into residence. I printed the wicked article and marched back to the immigration office, armed with knowledge, and a stern, confident poker face. I didn't ask anything, just stated that I wanted a document that proved my residency at my school's address as a foreign individual based on the purpose of studies. As if I was speaking a different language, the official promptly provided the necessary documents that I then submitted to my school so I could be officially accepted.

In retrospect, the solution was incredibly simple and something immigration officials should have known. Maybe they knew it, or it was something that would have taken them five minutes to look up.

However, people don't have five minutes for your problems when they don't have five minutes for themselves.

They might help, but you can't build your existence on the good will of others. You'll be out of control and constantly stressed out about the outcome. You'll be bound to someone else's mood, knowledge, or willingness to help.

"Freedom isn't free," states the common saying. Even though this saying was merely used to support the purpose of a war fought for the values of the country, it can be related to everyday life freedom as well. Your everyday freedom of choice and security has to be earned with sacrifice. This sacrifice might be in the form of taking the time to search for solutions by yourself, and accepting responsibility for yourself and what happens to you all the time.

How can you handle a challenge quickly, taking responsibility, without relying on the world to save you? I collected five questions you can ask yourself to properly address your problems without relying on others:

1. What is the challenge?

2. Why is it a challenge?

3. What do I know about the challenge? What should I learn about the challenge?

4. What is the worst case scenario?

5. What can I do to avoid the worst case scenario?

When you have answered these questions, start taking action. Step by step, you'll get to a solution.

This being said, I'm not trying to imply that people will never help you. Sometimes they will. Usually, they will expect something in return. To have the greatest peace of mind, however, you need to feel in control of your life. To feel in control, you need to understand your problems and know that you could be able to solve them, even if you outsource the solution to someone else.

For example, I hired an accounting company to deal with my paperwork. They are a firm with a good reputation and I chose them for that reason. Working with this firm, however, didn't prevent me from learning all that I could about accounting, taxes, and company management. I don't like to spend my time doing all the paperwork myself, but it gives me peace of mind that I can double check what my accounting firm is doing.

Key takeaway to discipline your mind:

Take responsibility for yourself because nobody else will.

People don't have five minutes for your problems when they don't have five minutes for themselves.

You don't have to solve all your problems by yourself. You can rely on others. However, the mere knowledge that you could solve your issues if you wanted to, gives you peace of mind.

Chapter 3: The Most Unreliable Organ

A few centuries ago, astrologists believed that Earth was in the center of the universe and everything else revolved around it. Even before that, the myth circulated about the Earth being cube-shaped and having a clear end line somewhere in the misty oceans. People once thought that they could heal different diseases by cutting someone's arm and letting it bleed. Some other people believed a short, black-haired man in Germany, who liked to spread hate when he said he'd build a superior nation made up of tall blonde people.

When I was a child, I believed my grandparents when they told me eating carrots would help me to whistle better, and my improved whistles would attract pigeons. (Apparently, when I was a kid, I really loved pigeons.) I also believed spinach made you stronger, but I resisted eating it to avoid getting disproportionately large forearms as Popeye did.

When I moved away from home, I told everybody that I was okay when in reality I was really lonely and afraid. I believed that winning someone's attention and love was something that could be bought, so I purchased clothes that made me fit in with my new environment. As a fifteen-year-old, I thought it was lame to be nice to others and showing disinterest was the way to win others' respect.

When I had my first boyfriend, I thought we'd always be together. We would have a little cottage in the woods, with lots of cats, and we'd be happy just being together. When he first cheated on me, I thought that I would never forgive him. When we broke up, I was certain I'd never love anybody as much as I loved him – and nobody would love me as he did. Then I had another boyfriend who loved me much more than I loved him. I thought I was responsible for his feelings and I felt guilty for not loving him more. I felt like a horrible person for not loving him as much as he loved me.

I was wrong all the way through - from the carrots to love.

I'm sure that if I look back five years from now to my thoughts today, I might feel that I was wrong. I hope I will. It means that I'll know more and be smarter in five years.

I don't even believe there is absolute right or wrong. There are things you experience to be right or wrong for you based on your values. Approaching it objectively, your freedom of practicing your righteousness expands to the point where you violate someone else's freedom in doing so. Not considering the extreme negative values (like those of the loud, short, black-haired German) that some people consider right, we can agree that "right" or "wrong" is largely subjective.

Based on their different experiences and values, people can have different answers to the same questions. None of those answers are inherently better or worse than another, as long as it doesn't harm someone else's freedom.

Our own answers might be different today than what we thought ten years ago. Many years ago, I was convinced that I should be mean to gain respect. Today I believe I was wrong back then.

Humans have a superpower, the ability to think. We think about our thoughts and emotions. Our brains work all the time. When we become puzzled about something, like what we should think about a situation, our brain starts to search through our emotional memory and fishes out a solution that we applied previously to a similar situation. This often gets us in trouble because each situation is different and would require a tailor-made response – especially in cases when we deal with different people.

For example, imagine that your ex cheated on you in a nasty manner by chatting on the phone with a lover. It is not uncommon that after a trauma like this, you'll be on edge whenever you see your partner typing on the phone, even when you are with a different partner. If you don't pay close attention to your thoughts, your brain on autopilot mode will release an emergency troop of emotions to deal with the threatening situation. Your new partner will find your lack of trust offensive and you'll end up having a fight. Reacting to unique situations with the same solution fished out from your emotional memory will cause you a lot of headaches. Our "brain problems" don't stop at the emotional memory responses.

The brain is a very fickle organ. It makes us believe we heard and saw things that weren't really there. It can even re-write our memory. For example, research has been done where people were shown holiday pictures in Disneyland where Bugs Bunny shakes hands with the kids. After the slideshow was over, some subjects clearly remembered shaking Bugs Bunny's hand as well, when they were in Disneyland, even though Bugs Bunny is a Warner Brothers character. Thus, he was never a character in Disneyland.[iii]

The faster you accept that your mind should be questioned from time to time, the better you'll become at making decisions. The better decisions you make, the better your life quality will be. Don't forget, I might be wrong with what I just said.

How can you question your beliefs?

Questioning your beliefs does not necessarily mean changing them.

When I was coaching people, I put great emphasis on my clients questioning their beliefs about themselves and their environments. I did this to help people question their beliefs in order to identify the ones that held them back from accomplishing their goals. It is a good start to find where, when, and from whom they learned the harmful beliefs. The questions I usually asked my clients were the following:

- When did you first start believing _____? (Whatever the belief in question may be.)

- Who taught you to believe that you _____? (Can or can't do something.)

- Did you ever question this belief? Did you ever conduct research to confirm the validity of the belief? Did you ask other sources to confirm the validity of your belief?

- How would it affect your life if you changed your mind on this belief? Would it affect someone else?

- Did you ever talk about this belief with someone who disagrees with it or has a different opinion on it?

These questions can help you to explore your beliefs and help you understand the beliefs of others in a constructive way.

You should question each of your most steadfast beliefs from time to time, because your brain learns, improves, and experiences novelty each day. If you really examine your beliefs under a microscope, you might discover that you are operating based on outdated beliefs. Questioning ingrained beliefs can be uncomfortable, but if you discover that they are no longer accurate, your life can improve for the better. For example, a person who used to be overweight may still operate based on his "fat self-image" related beliefs even after he loses a lot of weight. I had a client who lost a lot of weight and actually became quite fit and muscular. Still, for a long time, he acted very bashful and shy around women. He was surprised when women would talk to him and was convinced that they wanted something from him instead of being interested in getting to know him. It took my client a while to "slim his beliefs down" to his new body.

He used to be my patient and we worked together for a few months on his issue until he successfully updated his beliefs. If a person with a negative self-image can go from feeling that he is worthless to a belief like "I can make changes for the better," it can have a huge impact on his quality of life.

Questioning old, outdated beliefs can help in the fight against anxiety, too. For example, instead of anxiously avoiding women, my client was able to change his anxious belief by saying to himself, "I wonder how bad it would be if I went on one date with her."

Body Language

There is a discipline that can help you to figure out your own thoughts as well as the thoughts of others better. This discipline is the field of nonverbal communication, body language and the paralinguistic.

Based on Albert Mehrabian's research, nonverbal communications, body language and paralinguistic, account for up to ninety-three percent of the meaning that people receive from any human communication. Only seven percent of our understanding comes from the verbal expression itself.[iv]

Understanding body language gives us better awareness about the thoughts and feelings of fellow humans beyond our own assumptions. It can also help us to understand ourselves better. Our body language reveals our true feelings that our brain might want to otherwise conceal. For example, you can lie by saying you're not afraid of heights, trying to convince yourself and impress those around you. If your legs start to tremble, you involuntarily grip something, and you push your neck into your body or close your eyes often, your body language will clearly contradict your words.

If you send confusing signals to your partner, you can lose credibility, regardless if that person is consciously or subconsciously aware of it. When you meet somebody you haven't seen for a long time who welcomes you with a big smile but also has crossed arms and body turned towards the exit, you'll get the message that he's not as happy to see you as he claims.

Body language manifests your subconscious thinking, while words and thoughts indicate your conscious thinking. This doesn't mean your subconscious mind is "right." It is a pure emotion-driven auto responder system that relies on your previous experiences. The subconscious mind is where your instincts are housed, and regardless if it is right or wrong, at least it is honest. If you want to know the truth about what somebody thinks, pay more attention to their body language. That doesn't lie. You can also examine your own body language in situations when you're not sure exactly how you really feel.

People do not always say what they truly think or feel. If you want to get to the bottom of someone's real feelings, you have to discover what's behind their words. This book was not meant to be a body language manual, therefore I will mention just the main red lights to detect. If you want to broaden your knowledge about body language, I can recommend that you read Allan and Barbara Pease's books: *The Definitive Book of Body Language*, or *Signals*, or Joe Navarro's book *What Every Body Is Saying.*

Emotional hints can be detected easily. If somebody is crying, presumably the person is sad. But tears can also be ones of joy if they appear along with laughter. Some tears are used to gain sympathy; so in this sense, they are deceiving. Always examine the context for a more accurate assessment.

Emotions like anger, impatience, or anxiety are expressed through facial expressions and body language. Facial expressions are the easiest to read, followed by body language and body positions such as personal spacing. If a person holds his arms crossed in front of him while rhythmically tapping his foot, he probably is impatient. However, if he crosses his arms, looks downward, and awkwardly shuffles his feet, he is more likely anxious or embarrassed.

How can you determine a fake smile? The first sign of a true, heartfelt smile lies in the eyes. If someone is truly happy, not only will the lips curve upward but small wrinkles around the eyes will also appear. When we say "cheese" for the photographer, we seem to be smiling because the zygomatic muscles are pulled backward. Still, it will be a fake smile. Showing your teeth doesn't equate happiness in the animal world either. A monkey can be scared, happy or assailant if we take only its mouth's position into consideration. Its eyes help us tell the difference between the three feelings. The same is true with humans. If the eyes don't laugh, the smile isn't honest.[v] Just think about the Joker in The Dark Knight. He was smiling… and slicing people's throats in the meantime.

Oh, those telltale eyes. There are a lot of verbal expressions referring to certain nonverbal eye communication. "He looks down on me," "icy stare," "bewitching glance," "tell me in the eye," and so forth. The eyes are the mirror to the soul, some say. If you pay close attention, you can read many things from a person's eyes before they even say anything.

The eyes can be used as a manipulative device. Women often use the up-looking technique to convince men about something. (If you wonder what the up-looking technique looks like, Google Princess Diana's signature girl like glance photos.[vi] You know, where she shyly looks upward while keeping her chin down. True up-glance mastery…)

It is a common misbelief that liars hesitate to maintain eye contact. It is precisely because of this common notion that they usually have an unbreakable gaze. What can expose them is the twitching of their mouth, scratching their ears, and other out of context spasms of their limbs.

Before you make your final assessment of someone's body language, always consider cultural differences. Some signals are universally true everywhere, but some can be badly misunderstood. If you plan to travel, do a quick search for the typical praising or insulting nonverbal signs in the country you will visit. For example, Facebook's famous signature "Like" sign (the thumbs-up image) in the Western world means, "okay," "cool," "one," or a hitchhiking signal. In Greece, however, it means, "go to hell," especially if it is moved up and down. In Japan, it means "five" or "man."[vii]

How can you practice your body language reading skills?

Choose a good, old, black-and-white silent movie in a retro theater and try to predict what the characters will do next based on the emotions they seem to have, according to their mimics and gestures. Silent movies are excellent starters to observe body language because the lack of sounds forces the actors to be very expressive with their kinesthetic work. Thus their following actions are easily predictable.

When you can guess eight out of ten actions that follow in a silent movie, take your practice to the next level. Watch a normal movie with the sound muted. This will be much harder to guess what the character might do next because words and special effects normally help with predictability. When you can score eight of ten correct prognostications in muted "regular" movies, you can start reading the body language of the people around you.

Read the full body picture together. Don't jump to conclusions based on one or two signals, and most importantly, don't take your guessing for granted. Reading body language is just an additional craft that can help you discover other's feelings better than only relying on your thoughts or their spoken words.

Check your own body language occasionally and compare it to your conscious thoughts. Do they match? Don't forget, body language expresses the unfiltered feelings of your subconscious brain. You can learn a lot about yourself if you choose to pay attention to these subconscious signals.

Key takeaways to discipline your mind:

- Question your old, negative, outdated beliefs. Focus on finding out when, how, and who taught you this belief. Help yourself to change it by doing your own research on your belief's validity and ask people with differing viewpoints about it.

- Learn to read the most common body language signs. You can get a much clearer picture about how others truly feel.

Chapter 4: That Messy Stress

What is stress? Stress is your body's way of responding to any demand or threat.

When you feel threatened, your nervous system reacts by releasing stress hormones (including adrenaline and cortisol), which prepare your body for emergency action. Your blood pressure rises, your heart beats faster, your muscles tighten, and your senses become sharper. These changes increase your strength, enhance your focus, and speed up your reaction time.[viii]

What are the major causes of stress?

There are some external stressors like major life changes, school and workplace problems, financial difficulties, relationship struggles, and being overwhelmed in general.

Some stressors are internal, like having a negative self-image, worrying, perfectionism, a lack of flexibility, and thinking in extremes.

There are different types of stress levels.

Sub-stress – This is when you try to pretend that you don't care about things, and try to convince others (and yourself) that you are not stressed. Yet stress does affect you. You may not even realize it. Sub-stress is a very typical reaction of the "cool folks": "I don't give a flying... fig if people don't like me. Anyone who is important to me understands me. Others' opinions simply don't affect me..." To some extent it is good to not identify with the opinion of ill-wishers. But no one can be truly comfortable if most people dislike him or her. Pretending not to care is more like a comfortable mask to avoid taking responsibility through self-assessment, asking, "Why don't people like me in general?"

Optimal stress – This type of stress is helpful. It's the state when your body and mind are prepared to handle challenges. Your senses are sharp and you have optimal blood pressure to bring out your full potential. You are swimming in adrenaline.

If you manage to embrace this reaction of your body, you'll be able to empower your abilities. Your body usually shifts into this phase before a race, an interview, or a presentation. You dance on thin ice, though. If you don't control your state, you can easily fall into the next category, the supra-stress phase.

Supra-stress – This is the stress we hate. The one that paralyzes our brain, numbs our limbs, and makes us feel miserable. When we face supra-stress, life becomes a struggle. Experiencing supra-stress often can make us fearful of stress. We'll try to avoid stress at all costs to avoid the pain it causes. However, becoming anxious about avoiding stress is also a form of self-harm. The solution is not trying to cut all stress out of our lives, that's impossible. We need to change our attitude about it.

Supra-stress can be divided into three groups: manageable, partly manageable, and unmanageable.

Some sources of stress are unmanageable. You can't prevent or change stressors such as a serious illness, the death of somebody close to you, or a national crisis. In these cases, the best thing you can do it to accept them. It is not easy. But that's the only way to overcome it. Once you don't give power to stress but allow yourself to grieve, feel pain, or cry instead, the internal tension caused by stress will vanish.

Forgiveness and acceptance can ease the pain supra-stress causes. If you forgive yourself or others for something that caused you stress, you will feel a sense of relief as you are released from the stressful situation.

Partly manageable stressors are the issues that are partially caused by us. Since we have a certain amount of control over it, we can change our part in it.

For example, instead of continuously complaining about the office being a mood-killing environment, we can change it by decorating with vivid colors, flowers, and some pictures. If we don't like a colleague, we can decide whether to approach her differently from now on or to find a way to make her disinterested in us. In the worst case scenario, we can try to change departments or jobs. The most important thing is to eradicate the stressor that causes the damage from our lives.

Stressors that can be eradicated should be eradicated. Why? Because even if you control the anger the stressor generates, the poison stays inside you. You might not unleash your bitterness on the person who made you angry, but you will release the tension somewhere. Unfortunately, it will most likely be on someone who doesn't deserve it and has nothing to do with your stress.

Manageable stressors are all the first world problems like being late or not finding milk in the supermarket. This group is the most populated with thousands and thousands of little annoyances waiting to stress us out.

Stress—real or self-made—must be taken seriously because it can become the cause for physical and/or mental problems. Stress can inflict cognitive issues like memory problems, poor judgment, constant worrying, a negative world view, and concentration issues. It can also leave a mark in everyday behavior like causing eating and sleeping disorders, enhanced alcohol, drug, or cigarette usage, and other nervous habits like nail biting. The emotional symptoms of high stress are moodiness, having a short temper, feeling overwhelmed, an inability to relax, or depression. Stress can manifest in physical symptoms such as aches and pains, diarrhea, nausea, frequent colds, and a rapid heartbeat.

How can you handle stress better?

- First, identify your stressors.[ix]

Do your own research about your main stressors. Then identify the category in which your most frequent stressors fall: sub-stress, optimal-stress or supra-stress.

- When it comes to your supra-stress issues, determine which of your stressors are manageable, partly manageable, or unmanageable.

First, take care of your unmanageable stressors. Clearly, solving or erasing them is not an option. Ask yourself what you can do now to decrease the stress caused by the unmanageable stressor. Do you need to forgive someone? Do you need to accept something? What can you do to forgive or accept the stressor? Don't get me wrong. You're not doing this for someone else's sake. If your husband cheated on you, you don't forgive him so he can feel better. You forgive him so *you* can feel better; to be able to move on with your life and not waste your precious days in resentment.

If someone dear to you died, you accept it because, unfortunately, there is nothing else you can do. When my grandparents died, I felt a lot of sorrow and was angry at myself for not being more present during their last months. At some point, I decided that it was not helping anyone that I stressfully resented myself. My grandparents wouldn't have liked that either. Instead of wasting my breath on blaming myself, I did (and still do) everything I can to be more present in my parents' lives. Since then, I feel more at peace with myself. I still miss my grandparents, and will miss them forever, but I don't feel stress anymore. I gave myself space to truly grieve. That's a peaceful, bittersweet feeling.

- Social engagements can help you in reducing stress. [x]

Share your deepest fears with your friends. It will strengthen the bond between you.

However, don't complain too much, and don't use people just to free yourself from stress.

Have a stress journal. In the process of writing your issue down, you release some tension, and when you read your complaints over again a few days later, you will realize how trivial most of them were and how little of an impact they actually had in your life.

- R.E.S.T.: Relax, Eat, Sleep, Train.

Mens sana in corpore sano, a Latin phrase, is translated as "a healthy mind in a healthy body." It is much easier to face everyday challenges and stressors if you have a personalized healthy daily routine. Experiment with some sample routines and see what works best for you. Build R.E.S.T. in to your daily routine. If you want to train only twenty minutes and relax for three hours, it's up to you. As long as it fits into your schedule and you can meet your deadlines without stress, go for it.

• Pay attention to your feelings.

There is always a moment where the stress level is "optimal." After that it can turn into hurry, confusion, or mental blocking if you are not in control of your thoughts. Try to grasp that moment when the pressure is still optimal. It is the time when you still think about what you should do to perform at your best. The minute you start telling yourself that you won't succeed, you'll mess it up, and the optimal stress zone is gone.

When you face your next challenge, focus on finding your optimal stress zone. When you feel like you've got it, do not hesitate. Take action immediately. Don't let yourself fall into the jaws of supra-stress. If you can't take action immediately, because, let's say it is still not your turn to perform, keep yourself busy with something else. Go and talk to somebody or (I rarely say this) check your social media accounts.

- Learn to be patient.

Impatience often drags stressors into your life, most of the time avoidable ones. For example, at the post office, there are two lines, so you pick the shorter one. By Murphy's Law, the other line will move faster. So you decide to change lines. But fate chose to laugh at you that day, so from that moment, the line you previously stood in becomes faster. Then you decide to change again, and once again. If you had stayed in the line you originally chose, you'd already be done, walking in the sunshine and eating an ice cream cone. But you didn't because of your impatience. It is less stressful to stay in a line than to switch places and assume that the other line is faster.

Impatience causes stress, which can affect your mental and physical health in the long run. Impatience and anger are like drinking poison and expecting someone else to die.

When you are in a rush, after some minutes of torturous waiting, your nerves are tearing you up, stress hormones are ripping through your body, and your heart is beating like a delayed-action bomb. You start to imagine scenarios of the consequences of being late, praying for the line to move. But your agitation is useless. No matter the images your wild mind creates, you will still be stuck behind the customer with a cartload of groceries and coupons, on the bus next to the screaming child, or at a café with your friend who continues to discuss the same ongoing problem and you almost expire of fatal boredom.

Patience is a skill. It is not innate, but is learnable. If you take the time to acquire this skill, your life will be much easier. You will simply breathe more freely, knowing that stressors don't have any power over you anymore.

How can you become more patient?

First, find the triggers that flip your casual mood into impatience. Are these triggers people or certain words and behaviors? Is it the five o'clock rush hour? If you already identified your stressors in my previous exercise, it will be easier to select from those stressors that make you impatient. If you missed doing the exercise, this is your chance to do it now. What are your main stressors? Which ones make you impatient?

Becoming aware of what makes you impatient and why is a great start to changing it. Bringing something from the subconscious to the conscious mind helps you to take control over it.

Draw two columns on a paper. In the first column, write down something that happened today that made you impatient. For example, "my husband was so slow in telling a story," or "the waiter came late to take my order." When you are done listing your annoyances of the day, try to articulate why you lost your patience in each situation. Be honest. For example, "I lost my patience with my husband because I was in a rush and he decided to tell me his story right when I was about to head out," or "I lost my patience with the waiter because he took the order of people who got to the restaurant after me first."

Every time we lose patience, there is an unfulfilled need behind it. People and events are only the trigger, the stimulus of our impatience, never the reason. Nothing can make us impatient unless we allow it. The second step – after identifying our stressors – is to rephrase the cause of our impatience. As I said before, we lose patience because we have an unmet need behind it. Identify the need.

For example, what is the need behind this problem? "I lost my patience with my husband because I was in a rush and he decided to tell me his story right when I was about to head out." The unmet need in this case is the consideration of you being in a rush. You wished your husband was more sensitive and prioritized you not being late versus telling a story he could have told you later. Your lack of good time-management also fuels the impatience. You know you could have gotten up earlier to meet all your morning obligations in time.

If you let your impatience "speak" in this scenario, you'd say something like this to your husband, "Can't you see I'm in a rush? What's the point of this story? I feel you'll never get to the point." Hearing this, your husband will become defensive, he'll feel attacked and will not be interested in considering your needs, namely to wish you a good day and let you go to work. He'll start sulking or worse, pick a fight instead. Both of your needs will be unmet.

If, however, you address him patiently, focusing on your unmet needs versus his culpability, he'll be more likely to listen. "I'd love to hear your story later this afternoon, but right now, as you can see, I'm late for work. I need to get there on time so I won't be stressed out all day. It's my mistake that I didn't wake up earlier. I'll try to make it up to you by getting home twenty minutes earlier." In this case, your husband will not feel attacked or blamed. You acknowledged your own shortcoming in this situation, expressed appreciation for your husband's interest in spending time with you, and showed him a sign of good faith by promising to resume the talk in the afternoon. He probably would kiss you goodbye and you'd be heading off the next second. Both of your needs will be met; you'll get to work on time and he'll feel appreciated.

Let's take a closer look at the other situation: "I lost my patience with the waiter because he took the order of people who got to the restaurant after me first."

In this scenario, you needed to feel appreciated as a customer. The waiter taking others' orders first made you feel neglected, unappreciated, and maybe insulted. Analyze exactly what you feel. Diagnose the emotions rising in you and articulate what need of yours was unmet. I need to feel like an appreciated, respected customer. Telling the waiter "Hey, you. Don't you see I was here first? Take my order now!" will hardly win appreciation or respect. Lashing out at the waiter will sabotage both of your needs. The waiter's day will be miserable and he'll be resentful towards you which may cause you to end up with a substantial amount of spit in your pancakes.

If you approach the waiter saying, "Excuse me, I'm ready to order. I was here before those customers and didn't want to disturb you with my order earlier as I saw you were busy. However, I'm in a slight rush and I'd truly appreciate if you'd try to make sure my order gets done first. Thank you!" Staying calm, assuring the waiter that you are not mad, and showing interest in his work may win him to your cause. There is never a guarantee he can make sure your order gets done first, but he'll likely treat you with respect and be kind to you. You may or may not get your pancakes first, but you'll find your need met and will feel like an appreciated customer.

Now it's your turn to think of at least three events that made you impatient. Try to recall how you responded and write it down. Identify who you considered to be the cause of your impatience before. Realize that whatever or whoever that was, it was just the stimulus of your lack of patience. Then identify what unmet need really triggered the negative emotion in you. Rephrase your response in such a way that you focus on communicating your needs instead of blaming others.

After you're done with this exercise, assess it on a scale of one to ten, of how seriously the situation triggering impatience will affect you tomorrow? Next week? Next year? Chances are that by next week you'll have forgotten it completely, not to mention by next year.

Most "offenses" we experience are involuntary, in my opinion. People don't plot to make us feel miserable. We just fail to identify the need, the feeling that is unmet in us. It is always easier to blame our misery on others. Make an effort to be introspective whenever you lose your patience. When you feel the regular symptoms of impatience—heavy breathing, pounding heart, cloudy brain, clenching fists, agitation—take a step back. Take five deep breaths, find the need behind your impatience, and phrase your answer while focusing on your need.

If something inanimate makes you impatient that you can't address, like a traffic jam do the following exercise. Calm your breathing. Focus on something you are looking forward to or a pleasure from your past. Tension will slowly ease. Stay in this state. Do not let impatience take control over you again. Just relax and call whomever you should inform that you'll be late.

Patience training exercise: raise a flower or a small tree. Start with the state of seed or a little rooted branch. Water it as recommended, fertilize it, and take care of it. It is a good exercise to improve both your patience and your caretaking skills.

Key takeaway to discipline your mind:

- Become aware of your stressors. Realize that the stressors are only the stimulus of your stress and impatience. You are the only one who can control the interpretation of any stressful situation.

- Behind every impatient outburst there is an unmet need. Articulate this need and focus on it instead of culpability when you address your stressor.

Chapter 5: At Peace with Your Virtual Life

People are genuinely lazy. Think about all the inventions we've made—the washing machine, the oven, the car, and so on. All these inventions were brilliant, and they became successful because they simplified our everyday lives, helping us to have more time for other things. However, even if our lives are easier than our ancestors', we seem to find it harder to be appreciative.

What happened to our happiness?

According to studies, people today are much less happy. Anxiety disorder, mental illness, and depression is much more common than it was when everything was actually more depressing. We are obsessed with perfectionism: we want to have the perfect body, be perfectly happy, rich, funny, smart, witty, better – better – better. Be more productive, bring better results, post perfect pictures on social media about your perfectly nutritious breakfast, hop in your perfect car, and whistle happy melodies to get in perfect time to your perfect workplace.

Who has time to comply with all of these ideals of perfection? Nobody. Not even those who make a living promoting their perfect life on different sites. The idealized perfection we all chase does not exist. It's all fairy dust.

People invest so much time and energy to chase some utopist happiness vision where the sun always shines and bunnies jump around. Ironically, the more they invest in pursuing this vision of perfect happiness, the more disappointed they get. Why?

Because chasing perfection reminds them of their imperfections, inadequacy, and not being good enough.

For example, all the time you strive to have nicer hair you subconsciously know you do it because you think your hair has no volume and isn't shiny enough. It doesn't hit that invisible, superficial, crappy standard that a hair is supposed to meet.

Perfectionism is a weakness.

Consumer society is built upon exploiting this weakness. They sell you the idea that the road to happiness leads through a bigger car, better job, better-looking partner, more expensive clothing, or food. The keyword is more. Certain companies, clothing, and tools become status symbols and people, like sheep, start to baa, echoing the message of the commercials: *"my*

hair will look be-e-e-tter, I will be happier."
The problem is that you won't.

Why does social media affect us so much?

Have you ever posted something on social media and found yourself a little overly concerned with repeatedly checking in to see how many likes it received or what comments it was getting? If so, it turns out that you just might be... human.

Humans have always been social beings. We have been better together than on our own. It's part of our nature and it contributes to our survival and well-being. From the beginning of history, people have lived and traveled together because it isn't humanly possible to completely survive on our own.

From the Native Americans living in tribes near water sources so they could work together to hunt, fish, and offer each other protection, to the wagon trains of people traveling westward together to stay safe as they moved across the United States to their new homes, to families today that form neighborhood watches, carpool groups, and join together in community service projects, as well as everyone else in between, we have always wanted and needed to band together and sought to fit in and belong to a group.

Today, social media is no different. We are more connected than ever before and social media simply makes this connection more visible. There are dark sides of this overly opened and easy-to-follow virtual reality. Studies have been conducted warning us of the pitfalls of social media. They often point out that our self-confidence and self-esteem may be too tied to how we think people perceive us and our posts on social media.[xi]

There are some different opinions in the scientific field than of those experts who connect diminished self-esteem to social media.

While it is definitely important that we carefully monitor ourselves to ensure that our sense of self-worth comes from within and not just how many likes we receive on our social media accounts, psychologist Dr. Max Blumberg doesn't believe social media is completely changing the essence of who we are as some have feared. He believes that social media just makes the feelings and behaviors that have always been within us more noticeable.[xii]

Dr. Blumberg believes that how social media affects us depends a great deal on our individual personalities. Some people are more reliant upon external approval for their happiness than others. This has always been the case even before social media existed. He doesn't think that the prevalence of social media in our lives has made a greater percentage of the population insecure, it just has made their insecurity more noticeable because now they have a visible outlet to share their inner feelings that they didn't have before.

Dr. Blumberg points out that social media gives us a way to openly express ourselves and our inner thoughts and feelings. This is a chance we didn't always have. It's true that when we share things on social media, we do open ourselves up to the possibility that we will receive negative feedback from others, which can be scary, but we also open ourselves up to the possibility of receiving praise or positive feedback as well. He stresses that social media is like anything else in that it should be used in moderation.

Self-awareness is key. If we find ourselves being too concerned and consumed with checking our technical devices to see what others think of our posts, it is a definite signal that it is time to step back and take a break. While it is natural to be concerned to a degree about how others think and feel about us and to want their approval, it can't be where our whole identity and sense of self-worth comes from. We still have to be comfortable in our own skin – with or without social media in our lives.

Dr. Blumberg's viewpoint is food for thought worth considering. Today, the majority of people either emerge themselves in social media, or they hate it, reject it, and are very negative about it. Think about what relationship you have with your virtual reality. Make sure social media serves you and your best interest – not the other way around.

The relationship between the pursuit of happiness and social media

When you fail to accomplish something, you feel sad. Or bad. Or angry. That's okay. It is normal. The problem is that people think it is not normal. You start thinking that something's wrong with you. There must be. That girl could make the perfect hair picture and you couldn't. And she's happily sipping a rainbow unicorn cocktail in some club called The Billionaire while you sit at home munching some generic Nutella and watching a baking show. You think you're sad and boring, while everyone else out there is awesome. Seeing the greatest moments in other peoples' lives makes you think that your life is even worse than you thought it to be. Voilà, the cocktail for feeling inadequate and unhappy is ready to be served.

Whatever you see on social media is not real. At least not as real as you think. Social media is like a camera set on Mount Everest, and only takes a photo when you reach the peak. Everything that is below that point is unnoticed. If someone scrolls through your pictures, they will only see those moments when you reach the peak of the mountain, when you skydive and look good doing it (one in five hundred pictures), when you regained the beach body after giving birth. People will see only your best moments. But they will compare their regular life to those best moments. This is where the real danger lies. People know everything about their own memories – the good, the bad, the boring, and the ordinary – but only see your best ones. It is almost impossible to not feel inferior. What is the way out from this insanity?

Clear your thoughts and look at social media objectively. Whatever you see online has zero effect on your life. Even what you post has no effect on your life – you can post a smiley picture with teary eyes, you can claim to be happy while you really torture yourself with self-hating thoughts. It's not real – whatever goes on online. It does not affect reality. Focus on what matters, what has true impact on real life.

How can you ditch your social media worries?

Connecting too much of our sense of self-worth to the opinions of others, where it consumes a large part of our day, harms our self-esteem, and limits our happiness isn't healthy. If you find yourself too worried about how others think and feel about you, there are some things you can do to break free from this detrimental state of mind and take your power back.

- Remember that most people really aren't thinking about you nearly as much as you think they are. Everybody has their own problems and challenges to deal with every day. So with the notable exception of your parents, the vast majority of people do not have the time, energy, or inclination to devote a great deal of their time thinking about you, let alone judging you.

- Reclaim your power. Don't turn over your right to be happy to the opinions of others. You are responsible for you. No one has the power to ruin your day or stand in the way of you achieving your goals and dreams and living your best life unless you give it to them.

- Be okay with not knowing how others feel about you. We spend so much time worrying about what others think about us that we let it get in the way of living our lives. As long as we aren't hurting anyone else or standing in the way of their ability to live their lives, we should embrace the fact that it is our own choices and actions that determine our future and happiness. How others view us usually comes from their own experiences and events that have happened in their own lives over which we have no control and very little, if anything, to do with, so in the wise words of Queen Elsa from the movie *Frozen*, we will be best served to just "let it go" and stop worrying so much about the opinions of others.

- Focus on what really matters. Life is short. When we spend all of our time worrying what others think of us, we lose sight of the things that really matter. People will think what they think of you and there is often surprisingly little that you can do to change that. Despite your best intentions, there will always be people who will want to assume the worst about you. So instead of being held back and weighed down by them and their opinions, turn your attention to what you think of yourself. Stay true to who you are. Use your core beliefs and values as your compass, keeping you on the path to happiness and a life well-lived.

- Stop letting your fears control your life and make a plan. Human nature often causes us to live in the land of "what-if," where we assume the worst case scenario will always come true and it will have a lasting negative impact on our life. In fact, the worst case scenario rarely comes true, and even if it does, it even more rarely impacts our lives forever. Instead of constantly dwelling on and imagining all of the bad things that can happen if others don't like you or if you are rejected and don't fit into the group, redirect your thinking and make a plan. Say, "Okay, if the worst case scenario does come true, what are some strategies I can have in place for moving forward positively from it?" Just having a simple plan in place will go a long way toward putting things into proper perspective and alleviating your fears.

- Recognize and celebrate the fact that you are a work in progress. When you unfairly compare the ordinary moments in your life to the best moments in the lives of others displayed on social media, you can choose to react in one of two ways. You can let it get you down and be too hard on yourself, or you can take it as a chance to improve yourself.

We are all works in progress with plenty of room to learn, grow, and improve. If you find yourself comparing yourself to others, which at some point you inevitably will, look at it as a chance to grow and strengthen your self-esteem and the way you see yourself. Take a class, adopt a healthier lifestyle, spend more time surrounded by the people and things you love the most...live your best life. You'll have plenty of your own "best moments" to share with others on social media along the way.

Key takeaways to discipline your mind:

- Social media doesn't change the core of who we are, but it can certainly magnify the insecurities that exist within us. We need to be self-aware and monitor the way we are affected by the opinions others share about us on social media, and recognize when it is in our best interest to take a step back and focus on getting our sense of self-worth from within.

- Recognize that little on social media is exactly as it seems. Don't be so hard on yourself by unfairly comparing the ordinary moments of your life with the "best moments" people choose to display on social media. Understand that everyone has ordinary moments just like you and you should not feel inferior.

- Realize that everyone has their own problems and challenges to deal with which means they aren't thinking about and judging you nearly as much as you believe they are. Spend more of your time and attention on the things that really matter – improving yourself, developing your own identity and feeling of self-worth from within, and living your best life instead of worrying so much about the opinions of others.

Chapter 6: Choose One Thing and Dive Into It

There is something about you that makes you different from everyone else. No, it's not just your DNA. No, I'm not saying that you are more special than everyone else. You are just as special as the rest of us. But you have something unique, an ability, a skill, a trait; one thing that can make your life more meaningful. Some call it a purpose or calling; it's something you were born to do. A goal that can kick your mind into discipline. Something that's so important to you that you're willing to sacrifice every other career option for it. For Tiger Woods this is golf. For Steven Spielberg this is directing movies. For Bill Gates this is Microsoft. For you this is… you don't know it yet? It's time to start looking for it. When you find it, follow the path described below to bring out the most of it.

Steven Pressfield, the author of the bestselling book, *The War of Art*, differentiates two paths one can follow when it comes to doing or creating something: hierarchical orientation and territorial orientation.[xiii]

When someone follows the hierarchical orientation, he is in a constant fight with everyone else, always aiming to be first. His road is a constant battle with both those above him, and those beneath. His happiness and satisfaction will depend on his position in the hierarchy. If he reaches his expected position, he'll be happy for a brief period, if he doesn't he'll be sorrowful. Everything he does is done in order to meet his expectations and the expectation of others: how he dresses, acts, speaks, thinks, and what he creates. When we expect something for ourselves and we think hierarchically, Pressfield says, we "look up and look down. The one place we can't look is that place we must: within."[xiv]

Pressfield endorses territorial orientation over the hierarchical one. He claims that territory gives us a secure, safe place. Thinking within our territory will give us confidence and sustenance. A runner knows his territory is the running track. He knows what he can expect from himself there – he also knows that he can't expect to be his best self at costume designing. That's not his territory.

A territory can keep us going without external validation. In our territory, all we have to do is to put in our best effort and our territory will give back the fruits of our effort in the form of well-being and satisfaction. Our territory can only be claimed by hard work. LeBron James is not one of the best basketball players by chance. He put in a lot of effort in his territory. He practiced, he showed up every day, and he was present. He worked on developing his excellence and his territory returned exactly the amount of effort he put in. "A territory doesn't give. It gives back."[xv]

To check which field you operate on, hierarchy or territory, analyze what do you do in times of distress: do you call friends and relatives seeking reassurance, approval, and understanding, or do you immerse yourself in your thing? If you do the former, it means you're operating in hierarchical orientation. If you do the latter, it means that you're looking for calmness within your territory.

Pressfield provides another powerful question to help readers identify what territory they are on, "If you were the last person on earth, would you still do it?" If your answer is yes, it means you've found your thing and you're territorial about it. If Stephen King was the last person on Earth I bet he'd still write scary stories. He wouldn't do it to fit in a hierarchy (if he was the only one left, hierarchy would lose its meaning anyway), he'd do it for the sake of self-expression and self-entertainment. He would write purely because he loves to unleash his creative genius.

Did you identify yourself as acting hierarchically or territorially? Would you do your thing in sorrow and distress? It doesn't matter if you are a designer, a mother, a mechanic, or an artist. Would you do your thing no matter the circumstances? If yes, you know that you have found your thing. If not, search further.

To have a disciplined mind, you can't allow yourself to be distracted by many little temptations. Dividing your time and attention among many things will lead to achieving mediocre results in all of them. If you are comfortable with these mediocre results, there is no problem. But as we read in the previous chapter, people can rarely settle for mediocrity. They aim for excellence. They set their expectations high. When they set high expectations in many things but they fail to meet them, they will feel an internal conflict. Unmet expectations create a lack of confidence, low self-esteem, sorrow, disappointment, and a loss of faith in one's abilities.

When I was younger and was still searching for my one thing, I invested myself in chasing multiple goals. When you don't know what your one thing is, it's okay to try more things out. You shouldn't attach any other expectation to them other than helping you find your one thing. When you find it, become territory oriented and start working hard on your field. I identified writing to be my "one thing." Ever since then I quit all of the other distractions in my life and I now focus all my energy in this one thing. I compete with myself and myself only. I aim for quality and value the less instead of more. I started saying no instead of yes, to not allow myself to get derailed from my path. I stopped reaching for confirmation on social media. I only look for feedback for the sake of improving.

Did it hurt to make this change? Hell yeah. I felt horrible when I chose to quit things I had worked on for months. I felt really sad when I decided to quit coaching. Refusing someone's request for help made me feel terrible. However, those tough decisions had to be made to clear my schedule and focus on my chosen field.

Changes hurt. It is perfectly normal. You're acting against your old values. You're acting against your "more mindset." It is scary to settle for one thing. The subconscious brain perceives this change as an attack against the cherished old, well-accustomed habits and tries to annihilate the danger. How? By making you feel pain and doubt. Loss, fear, anxiety, guilt – your subconscious brain has an entire arsenal of negative emotions to unleash to protect your old values. Pressfield, however, identifies these things as excuses that try to sabotage the real path that was meant for you. He calls this self-sabotaging power "resistance."[xvi]

There is a great power in embracing pain and acting against it. The biggest character-shaping moments in your life are those negative lessons that you can use to your benefit. Trying to avoid them equals trying to avoid improvement. Avoiding pain is painful. Avoiding struggle is a struggle. Avoiding settling for the one thing that was meant for you will always cause you internal conflict – and a dissatisfied mind.

Let's get real here for a moment. Your life will end. My life will end, too. There are limited things we can care about, pursue, or value during our lifetime. And while all this might seem obvious, in the heat of the moment it is not that easy to prioritize and focus your thoughts on the one thing that is really worth your time. Some people find it in childhood, others die trying to find their purpose on this Earth. Colonel Sanders passed his 60th birthday mark when he found his one thing. It is never too late, you know. Here are some directives you can consider once you find your thing:

> 1. Don't wait for the "right moment" or the "perfect conditions" to start what you feel you're meant to do. Do it now.

> 2. Keep a journal of the achievements you reach doing your thing. Hang them up as a constant visual reminder that

you're on the right track and you're progressing.

3. Organize your living area to help you in doing your thing.

4. Exclude time and energy thieves from your life.

5. Focus on those activities that help you develop your thing.

6. You call it multitasking, I call it a distraction. Do one activity at a time.

7. Allow yourself to be "lost." Turn off your cell phone, turn off the Wi-Fi, and dedicate all your attention to who and what matters the most to you.

8. Hydrate yourself. You do? Drink more. I'm serious. Nothing can be as sneakily distracting as dehydration.

9. Be grateful for what you have. Focus on that instead of complaining about what you don't have.

10. You can have more "one things" during a lifetime. If you know you were meant for multiple things, do them all just not at the same time. Dedicate a decade to mastering each of them.

Finding purpose in your life is a secure way to discipline your mind. When you have a personal goal to fight for, to dream about, and to look forward to, your mind won't have time to wander aimlessly. This something should be about you, and you alone. This one thing is not to be shared with anyone, this is yours. It is for you and about you.

Key takeaway to discipline your mind:

- Find one thing that defines you, that you can call your purpose, and focus your mind on it. Don't let your mind divide its attention on many things that don't make you fulfilled.

Chapter 7: Self-Knowledge

"Who am I? What's my purpose? How can I become a better…?"

These questions circulate in our minds on a daily basis. Oddly enough, one day we feel we know the answers, the next day we question them, and on the third day we're totally lost again. But in fact there is nothing weird about this. Our brain is evolutionarily developed to question everything, including itself. The constant questioning, however, leads to some distress in life.

I don't think there is a clear and long-term answer for the questions above because we change so often. If you asked me who I was and what my purpose on this Earth was fifteen years ago, I would have answered, "I'm the girlfriend of my (now ex-) boyfriend, and my purpose is to get married to him and grow chickens and farm together." Today this answer sounds hilarious – the chicken part much less than the others.

Psychologists have found that the stories we tell ourselves about who we are seriously affect our behavior, whether in a positive or negative sense. If you believe that you are smart, you actually achieve better results on mental challenges, tests, and in arguments. I conducted my own mini experiment to demonstrate this theory. I once gave my grandpa two pills for his headache. After he told me that he felt much better I revealed to him that I had actually given him Tic Tacs instead of medicine

Our beliefs have power over us. This is precisely the reason why we should be aware of them and learn to question them over time.

Zen Buddhism differentiates two types of mind: the thinking mind and the observing mind. The thinking mind is the voice in your head that relentlessly chatters. Even if you decide to meditate and quiet your thoughts, it will still project some pictures and thoughts. The thinking mind never sleeps: it talks to you when you stand in line, when you're about to sleep, sometimes even in your sleep. Have you ever noticed this? Yes? Then you did it with your observing mind.

The observing mind is the one you use to keep track of your thoughts and actions. Unfortunately, people don't use their observing minds as vigorously as they do their thinking mind. Until I read about Zen Buddhism, I didn't even know this distinction existed.

Instead, I called my observing mind my better judgment or my right mind while I often referred to the thinking mind as being "out of my mind." I usually wasn't in my right mind. When someone cries out to you, saying, "What were you thinking? You're not in your right mind!" that person actually means, "Hey, doofus! Please check on your thinking mind with your observing mind because it's running wild!"

When the thinking mind gets out of control, the observing mind can't do much about it. Have you ever asked someone for help on how to channel your anger? "What can I do to stop feeling angry?"

The answer is, you can't stop it. Once the thinking mind is unchained, that horse is gone. What you can do is to not identify with your emotions. Zen teaches that instead of telling yourself "I am angry," say, "I feel anger." You are not the human form of anger, you were just poisoned by this emotion. By making this tiny switch in your thinking, you can separate yourself from the emotion.[xvii]

Your emotions pop up from your subconscious, you can't control them. But you can control how you express them. As soon as you become aware of the mess your thinking mind is about to cause, you can catch yourself in the moment, accept that you feel anger, or fear or anxiety, and consciously take them under your mental microscope.

Anger, just like impatience, arises because of an unmet need. It can be your unmet need or the unmet need of someone else.

For example, you can feel anger whenever you're trying to talk to your partner and he doesn't seem to listen. "It's like talking to a statue," you may think. If you take your real feelings under the microscope, you might realize that anger is just a secondary feeling. What you truly need is to be heard and to feel understood. Instead of communicating to your partner that "you're like a statue, it's impossible to talk to you," try saying, "It would make me very happy if you listened to me. I need to feel connected and understood" (or whatever need you are covering with anger).[xviii]

Sometimes we become angry because someone else is hostile toward us or a cause we believe in. In this case, it can be helpful to listen and figure out what the unmet need is behind the other person's anger. If your partner says you have emotional constipation you have the following choices: you can hate yourself for being so emotionless (and believe what your critic says), you can feel resentment toward your partner for saying something so hurtful, or you can choose to examine what you feel and why you find his remark painful, while thinking about what unmet need of his is causing him to make such a remark. For example, you may find his remark painful because you feel unappreciated for all of your efforts when you do try to be emotional. You can also empathize with your partner, who may need more emotional feedback from you and right now is unhappy. Instead of lashing out at him, saying, "You are such a jerk and what you said is very unfair," you can say something like, "Thank you for being honest with me. I acknowledge that you say this because you feel the need for more emotional feedback from me. I wish to tell you that although I accept your need, your remark made me feel unappreciated and sorrowful because it implies you don't recognize the effort I make when I am emotional."

You don't have the power to avoid feeling anger, but you do have the power to decide how you will express it. Marshall B.

Rosenberg, in his book *Nonviolent Communication,* gives a very good summary on how to communicate different negative emotions peacefully. If you'd like to read more on this topic, I highly recommend his book.

Separate your emotions from your identity. You are not your emotions. The more you choose to focus on your emotions, the more powerful they become. Even if you focus on getting rid of negative emotions, they'll have a greater presence in your life the harder you try. Also, focusing on something you don't want to do is much less effective than focusing your attention on the things you want to do. For example, instead of saying "I don't want to feel anger," say "I want to feel peaceful."

Accept that negative thoughts and emotions are part of life. You can't get rid of them, but you can let them go. Stop identifying with them. Change negative statements like "I hate my job" to "I'm feeling hatred towards my job." This way you gain a verbal and mental distance from the problems. You will realize that your rephrased negative statements are suggesting a temporary state instead of an unchangeable fact.

Self-Discipline

If the upgraded version of Toyota is Lexus, the advanced version of patience is self-discipline. Well-founded self-discipline can grant you long-term success in all aspects of life.

It doesn't matter if you wish to be slimmer, a better football player, or an acknowledged performer, self-discipline is the number one quality you need to achieve your goals.

Studies show that people with greater self-control are happier because they can handle difficult situations better. Crisis periods are shorter in their lives, and they are able to make positive decisions more easily and rationally.

Self-discipline is a learned quality, just like patience. It doesn't come naturally, but with concentration and effort, it can be developed. Offering great long-term benefits, self-discipline will help you to make wiser, healthier choices; you learn to control your emotions, so when you make a decision, it will be less influenced by them.

What's the difference between patience and self-discipline?

Mark's friends called him to say they were running late and wouldn't make it to his place sooner than 6:00 p.m. Mark was a patient guy and he didn't make a fuss about the delay. He sat down and looked around the table. There were lots of sweets and sandwiches prepared for the afternoon with his friends. He thought he should indulge himself with one bite or two while waiting. The candies were delicious, so he ate another one and another. Even though he knew he had a weight problem, he couldn't stop eating to make the time pass.

What's the lesson in this simple story? Mark had developed the quality of patience, so he didn't argue with his friends for being late. But he couldn't stop eating even though he wasn't that hungry. He lacked self-control, which is the foundation of self-discipline.

The easiest way to start practicing self-discipline is to apply the rule "out of sight, out of mind." Self-discipline is all about acknowledging your temptations and refusing to let them control you. A temptation might be a bad eating habit, as in Mark's case, or something like the inability to switch off the phone when you're in the middle of a major project.

If you exercise self-discipline, your conscious mind will be powerful enough to keep you from giving in to these temptations, even if they are in front of you. However, I'd suggest you exclude them from your environment in the beginning.

Mia had weight issues, so one day she decided to start a very strict diet. She could eat a low-carb meal only once a day, and drink some protein shakes throughout the day. She admired how self-disciplined she had become to reach this higher level of self-control. But at the same time, she became moody, she often lost focus, and her ability to concentrate decreased noticeably. Basically, she lost control of everything but the diet.

Self-discipline shakes when your Maslow pyramid crumbles.[xix] Balance your eating and drinking habits to be able to maintain your discipline. If your basic human needs are not satisfied, you won't be able to follow your plans in a disciplined and patient manner. Provide the necessary nutrition to keep your brain on track. If your blood sugar is regulated, you'll have better focus, and you'll go on through your day in a more productive way.

Remember, being comfortable is not your primary goal. If you decide to use your self-discipline to change old habits, a sensation of discomfort will inevitably hit you. Trying to preserve the status quo is a natural reaction from your brain. The brain doesn't like changes, the comfort zone is its normal state and everything that threatens this comfort, the brain tries to eliminate. If it sends you the feeling of discomfort or pain, your brain is betting that you will stop trying to change things and get back to normal.

However, if you are disciplined enough and you persist, your brain will begin to accept your new habits and create a new comfort zone. Habits don't stick quickly and easily. If you lose control and act without being disciplined, forgive yourself for that. When you decide to do something differently, change won't come instantly. You will have some low-points. You will have rough patches even in your disciplined life; you're not a machine after all. Self-discipline's purpose is not to turn you into Buddha himself, but to help you to think clearer, be in control of your life, and choose your battles wisely.

Learning to say no to others is where self-awareness starts. Learning to say no to yourself is where self-discipline starts. Do you want to achieve something? Dump the excuses, step onto the right path *today* and unwaveringly commit yourself to staying on it!

"Discipline is the bridge between goals and accomplishment."

- Jim Rohn

Key takeaways to discipline your mind:

- Learn to be patient. Notice the unmet needs behind your anger or the anger of someone else. Focus on addressing these needs instead of blaming yourself or others.

- Cultivate self-discipline. Keep your basic needs satisfied (eat well, drink and sleep enough) so you won't sabotage your discipline and focus.

Chapter 8: Don't Attract, Act

Have you ever wanted something badly, and somehow you got it but you really didn't understand how? The only explanation you could find was that you "attracted" it with the power of your thought.

The human mind is truly tremendous. It has the power to create the greatest companies in the world, but it can also be used to destroy. Whatever you think about creates your reality. That's why I always warn myself, "Be careful of what you think, because one day it may come true."

The things you experience in your outside world have their origin in your inner world. In other words, all the circumstances of your life are the consequence of your beliefs, and this is true for every aspect of your life. Your thoughts affect the state of your health, relationships, and finances. Look around you. Whatever you see—good or bad—is the result of your mental creation.

If you don't like what you see or experience, change your thoughts. It is this simple. People think that if they change their hairstyle, their life will also change. Nope. True change happens inside the head, not on the outside.

How can you become more conscious about your thoughts?

Most of us go through the day with very little notice of our thoughts. We usually don't examine how our mind works. We are often not aware of what causes fear in us or what small talks we mentally have with ourselves during the day. We eat, work, shop, plan, talk, play, and flirt but hardly ever examine our thoughts about these actions.

Do this exercise every day: for a few minutes, examine your thoughts about certain actions you are taking. You know, like, "Now I'm going to the kitchen to pick a soda," or, "I'm so angry about the payment delay at my company, I attract this kind of misfortune." Pay attention to your thoughts related to everyday actions just as much as you do on the significant things.

What you focus your mind on, that's what you'll attract. I'm sometimes skeptical of the whole law-of-attraction idea, but I can't deny that some things come in inexplicable ways.

What we call the law of attraction has more to do with self-awareness. When we're in a foul mood we really don't look around ourselves. We are so gloomy and consumed with our own problems that we miss our opportunities along the road. That's why we don't "attract" anything good with a negative mindset – because the mind is closed and clouded.

When we are carefree, living in the present, full of hope and stopping to smell the proverbial roses, we find that dime in the street, we'll notice that call for a job, we'll participate in that competition. And guess what? Just by opening up, participating, and being kind and likable, we'll attract positive things in our lives. It's not some giant conspiracy act of the Universe, it's all just you acting differently.

The power of thought in Zoeland is nothing more and nothing less than what you physically bring out of your thoughts.

I have a friend who is obsessed with the law of attraction. He read all the books by Rhonda Byrnes and he practiced the laws diligently, but he got the wrong end of it. Recently his favorite pastime is to attract buses. I'm not joking. It is thanks to him that I became familiar with the law of attraction in the first place. One time, years ago, we were going somewhere. Suddenly he stopped, lifted his pointer finger as if a eureka idea hit him, clenched his eyes shut and struggled so profoundly to concentrate that his forehead got more wrinkles than a shar-pei. "Did you just fart or something?" I asked.

"No," he replied, "I just channeled the Universe to send us the bus right now."

I was not interested in self-help back then. In fact, I was more Earth-bound than the wildest stockbroker on Wall Street. You can imagine my disbelief and bewilderment, especially after I made sure he actually meant what he said. I took a few safe-distance steps and patiently waited for the bus that showed up a few minutes later. ("Your negative thoughts chased it away. That's why we had to wait for so long," was his explanation.)

My friend achieved one thing though. Even if he didn't teleport a bus for us in the next thirty seconds using his mental Jedi powers, he made me curious about what on Earth could turn him into the Obi-Wan of busses. I bought *The Secret*, my very first self-help book. Now that I think it through, he is the indirect reason I'm writing this book right now. Without him and his bus, I might have never opened my mind to write in this genre. However, I always wanted to become a writer. Was this a huge conspiracy of the Universe and I was still blindfolded in front of its power?

Or rather, was it me catching an interest in the topic, and while digesting it with a pinch of salt, I worked and read a lot, to be able to put my own self-help thoughts together in a book and deliver it to you? I leave this question open for you to answer.

"Weak is he who permits his thoughts to control his actions; strong is he who forces his actions to control his thoughts." Og Mandino

Your brain can focus on only one thing at a time. Make that focus point a constructive one. To change your external conditions, you first have to change your internal ones. Train your conscious mind to stay open and be success oriented, rather than pondering on what's not good. Keep your mind busy with good expectations and act upon them, and soon you'll see that you'll attract the desired things. Not due to some cosmic conspiracy but yourself.

If you learn to act in your best interest, you won't need to murmur spells to attract good results. One thing you should believe in is the fact that you deserve whatever you're trying to achieve. I don't mean you should feel entitled, just feel worthy of getting what you wish for.

Why? If you feel unworthy of something, you won't be able to act in your best interest to get it. You'll think that your object (or subject) of desire is too good or too difficult for you to have. As a result, the "Universe" will never give it to you, simply because you gave up on acting resiliently to get it.

If you want to get a job in design and you feel worthy of that position, you'll polish your resume, you'll promote yourself fearlessly, you'll send out your work samples from the smallest to the biggest companies, and you'll constantly work to improve your design skills. One lazy Friday morning you'll wake up and get an interview appointment from a great company. Was it the Universe? Sure, because you increased and spread your chances around in the Universe. You acted in your best interest and the Universe replied.

If you believe in the law of attraction, please ignore my skepticism. Go on with attracting whatever you want: buses, money, or your better half. Please add to your attraction some constructive actions, too. You know, it is like the lottery – to have the chance to win, you need to buy a ticket. We have this saying in Hungary, "Help yourself and God will help you, too." I think this saying can be applied to the law of attraction too, just change God to the Universe.

Key takeaway to discipline your mind:
Believe first and foremost in your efforts. Whatever you wish to get in life, you have a better chance of getting it if you walk around with an open mind. Take steps that help you to get closer to your wish; don't attract, act.

Chapter 9: Failing and Learning

He who ran away from his family early, lied about his age to become an ambulance driver, who was fired from a newspaper for "lacking imagination and having no good ideas", who started and failed a cartoon series in Kansas City, who started several other businesses and failed, who drew an excellent mouse character and got it rejected because it scared off women, who lost his mother in a carbon dioxide accident in a house built to offer her a better life, whose workmen left to fight the Second World War, that transformed his studio into a tank repair artillery, who had a four-million-dollar debt, who struggled to open his first funfair for family entertainment was Walt Disney – a person we regard as the symbol of ultimate success.[xx]

Despite our best efforts, failure and pain invades our lives from time to time. It doesn't matter how self-disciplined, focused, or positive we are, failure is an inevitable component of life.

This being said, there is no better teacher in life than failure. True greatness mounts on a multitude of tiny and big failures. If you know someone who is very good at what she does, she went through a lot of failures to get there.

When you learned to talk, you mispronounced some words, you babbled, and sometimes you confused words and meanings. Still, you didn't give up until you learned to talk. As a child, you never thought that maybe talking wasn't for you and never said a word again.

Ironically, most of your failures come from bad standards you set for yourself. For example, if you say, "I want to be the smartest on my team," that puts you in a fragile position where you lose control over the situation. You can't control how much others study or how talented they are at presentations. You'll be anxious, constantly in a fight with the world, and dependent on others. You chose a bad standard to measure up to. If you choose instead to say, "I want to improve my presentation skills from good enough to very good," you'll be able to reach your standard without failing, regardless of how others perform. You'll be in control.

Set your standards within your "control zone" to stop exposing yourself to unnecessary avoidable failures.

Failure is a feeling that we all interpret in the same way, more or less. It is the devastating feeling of loss, anxiety, and sadness. The difference between us is how much time each of us needs to get over a failure.

Some of us appear to magically deal with failure and will even smile the next day. Many toss and turn for weeks, contemplating why it happened. Others feel the need to talk about it all the time; while in contrast, some don't say a word with an apathetic stare. Sometimes people become angry if you try to help them after a failure.

Generally speaking, you shouldn't take failures personally. Just because this time you didn't succeed, it doesn't make you a failure. In fact, this kind of event helps you to become more persistent, self-disciplined, and wise. This is why it is crucial to approach failure analytically.

Ask yourself these questions:
- Why did I fail?
- What actions might have brought about a better outcome?

- Was the failure completely beyond my control?
- After gathering the facts, take a step back and ask: what did I learn from this?

Sometimes we are not as bothered by the failure itself as we are by what others might say about our misfortune. Let it go. Those who will identify you by your failures are insignificant people.

Don't try to hide your failure. Taking a brave step of acceptance can bring you more respect than trying to sweep it under the carpet.

Success doesn't come for free. But it tastes so much better when we reach it. So embrace failure, make peace with it, and learn and grow from it.

Make peace with your previous failures if they still haunt you. Go to a place where you experienced a significant failure a few years ago.

It can be your old school, a sports center, a workplace… anywhere. I personally went back to a Burger King restaurant, to a specific table where I had my very first breakup. When this event happened, I thought it was the end of the world, and that I would never be okay again.

For a few years, I avoided that place like the plague. But one day I decided to go back. I bought a burger and sat at the table. I was expecting to feel some sort of cathartic moment of liberation, but I felt nothing. I was long over it. I just nonsensically clung to the pain. Going back and having this realization was the moment when I could let go of my personal failure for good, keep the lessons learned, and move on.

Facing a place where you once had a negative shock in the past can be sobering. Once you see that nothing is left there that remembers your pain, shame, or disappointment, you can heal. To leave the past and pain behind for good, write on a piece of paper every bad, sad, infuriating, unjust, painful, damaging feeling and thought you had at the place where you are. Tear the paper apart, burn it if you can do so safely, bury it, throw rocks at it, anything that will release you from any tension you still have.

When you're done, leave.

What are you holding on to that's holding you back? Did some people have a bad influence on you? Did somebody hurt you, cheat on you, or mistreat you? Do you feel frustrated about something?

What's the first step you need to take to let it go?

Cry it out—loudly and openly. If you keep it in, it can manifest in physical illness. Engage in a new activity. Learn a new skill or just introduce a physical habit into your life. Turning your focus to something new and enjoyable can build a bridge between a bitter past and a promising future.

Do you feel anger? Don't try to avoid this feeling; rather, feel it fully. If you try to hide it or keep it in, it will burst out inevitably and may hurt innocent people. Then remind yourself that nothing lasts forever and neither will anger. Try to find what need hides behind your anger and where your responsibility lies.

Are past relationships holding you back? Try to stop romanticizing the bond and face the facts. Make an unbiased list of good and bad things you experienced in this relationship. It will help you to see that more things weigh on the negative side, and that's why the relationship ended in the first place.

There are always bigger fish... and a better love. Don't make the mistake of convincing yourself that nobody will love you as much as the other person did. Do your best to love yourself as much as possible. When you learn to love yourself, you won't need the emotional validation from others so badly.

Know that when the rain is over, the sun will always come out. If you know that something good will follow, you'll let go much easier.

My dad told me a story when I was lovesick. In ancient India, a girl asked her father to give her a gift for her birthday that would raise her spirit in times of sorrow, and bring her back to Earth where she is head over heels. The father acknowledged her request. For her birthday, she received a medal on which four words were engraved: "*it won't last forever.*"

Key takeaway to discipline your mind:

- When you fail, don't hide from it. Accept it and allow yourself to feel the pain. Then talk about it, stop romanticizing it, and harness the lessons you can learn from it. Remember, neither pain nor success will last forever.

Chapter 10: Practice, Practice, Practice

Repetition is the mother of knowledge, people say. "Life itself is one long practice session. Everything in life worth achieving requires practice," noted the author of the book *The Practicing Mind*, Thomas M. Sterner.[xxi]

When we talk about practice, people tend to associate it with practicing a sport or on a musical instrument. There are more things in life that require practice, like developing patience, improving communication skills, and adopting meditation, among others. Sterner argues that one's true goal should be maintaining the practicing process instead of strictly focusing on the outcome. He states that being process-oriented and present will pave the path to self-discipline, sharp focus, patience, and self-awareness.

When my mom married my dad, she quickly found that she had some big shoes to fill. My dad was a big fan of his mother's cooking. My mom told me stories of how she would try to recreate my dad's favorite home cooked meals to show her new husband that she too could be a good cook.

This seems like a simple problem to solve, right? My mom went to my grandma to ask if she could have some of her recipes – especially her famous oyster dressing recipe she makes every Thanksgiving. The problem is, my grandma didn't believe it was important to write down recipes. She just cooked by "feel."

My mom told me of how she followed my grandma around the kitchen, watching her and writing down her every word. This was once again more complicated than you might expect, as my grandma didn't measure her ingredients and often said to add "a pinch" of this or that.

My mom spent many Thanksgivings trying to get the recipe just right. Finally, after much practice, she had perfected it, much to the joy of both her and my dad. My family makes this recipe for oyster dressing every year and it serves as a testament to the cooking skills of both my grandma and my mom, as well as my mom's perseverance.

Don't make the mistake of thinking that only artistic aspirations or work related things require practice. Everything we wish to learn and improve in our lives require practice; raising a child, learning to budget, to plan the perfect trip.

This sounds overwhelming, right? It seems that all of our twenty-four hours are a practice session. Yes and no. There is a trick in this equation. This trick is called priorities. Choose your preferred territories (goals) where you want to experience great rewards for your great efforts, then roll your sleeves up and steadily start working towards these goals.

The difference between practice and learning

Many of us associate the concept of practicing with the concept of learning. They may seem similar but Thomas Sterner, author of the book *Practicing Mind,* explains that "practice" and "learning" are not the same. "The word "practice" implies the presence of awareness and will. The word learning does not."[xxii]

"Practicing" something requires intention. We repeat something deliberately to reach a goal. Through repetition, knowledge sinks in, thus practice involves learning. But learning does not involve practice necessarily. When you choose to practice something by choice, you're in the present moment. You're inside the movement. Arnold Schwarzenegger described his weight trainings in his book *Total Recall* as being a form of meditation.[xxiii] He said when he trained a muscle group, he was mentally inside the muscle, feeling it, observing it, talking to it, telling it to grow. He was focused, he was present, he was practicing – and learning. He was not judging himself, he was simply executing an activity, observed the results, and adjusted himself for better future practices to reach his goal.

While the outcome shouldn't be your sole objective, you can use it as a motivator to improve your practice. Avoid using your goal as an indicator of success or a measurer of self-worth. Just focus on mastering yourself by practicing, doing the best you can right now.

When you are focused and productive, you'll have a peace of mind at night, even if you didn't reach your goal but did all you could for the day. When you are unfocused and procrastinating, even if you finish what you want for the day, you'll feel that something is missing. That something is missing out on being your best self.

The disciplined mind rejects instant gratification.

Why do we procrastinate if we know and feel sometimes consciously, sometimes subconsciously, that it is bad for us? Because in the heat of the moment, the pain of doing what we should seems greater than doing nothing. In other words, we choose instant gratification; a short term satisfaction that never has lasting value.

With practice and awareness you can learn to ditch the seduction of short-lived pleasures. After all, how many things can you recall in your life that you reached with little or no effort and made a great impact on you? Now try to recall things for which you worked diligently and patiently over a longer period of time. Was it easier? Were/are these hard things more valuable to you? Whenever you achieve something through effort and hardship, you experience a joy and satisfaction that easy and quick nuggets can never give.

For example, when I was a young child I could have easily abandoned my studies to enjoy the instant gratification of playing with my friends or playing a video game, but a high value was always placed on education in my family, so I kept my focus more on my long-term goal of doing well in school. Ultimately, my focus earned me a scholarship abroad. I was always certain to complete my school work before I played and I earned very good grades. It was by postponing instant gratification in favor of delayed gratification that I was able to earn scholarships to pay for my education and pursue my higher dreams for my life. I am forever grateful that my parents instilled those values in me and I learned to make choices like that in my life.

A disciplined mind notices when it falls out of the present moment.

If you ever practiced meditation, you know that its main goal is to help you stay in the present moment as much as possible. Thoughts will invade your practice and that's fine. The goal of meditation is not achieving thoughtlessness but noticing the thoughts and then returning the focus to the present moment; usually to the breathing.

If you have practiced meditation for some time, your mind will not only notice thoughts arising during the practice but also feelings during your day. Whenever you are feeling impatient, angry, rushed, bored, sad or disappointed with yourself, you'll be able to bring your awareness to these feelings. You can also notice that these feelings are not about the present moment – they are usually driven by anxiety for the future or remorse for the past. This means, whenever you notice these negative feelings arising, in fact you left the present moment. Notice where your mind and energy has drifted, where your focus is. Acknowledge the negative feeling. Say, "hello fear, or anxiety, or anger, I can see you. I notice you and let you go." Then gently take a few deep breaths and come back to the present moment.

When you are practicing something, it's only worth doing if you are in the here and now. That's when and where the knowledge absorbs, that's how you get the greatest return on your time investment. When you are practicing well, you are not aware you are practicing well.

Mastering present moment awareness is a life-long process. It's not a skill to brag about though. You don't make the great effort of practicing being in the present to put on your resume, "I'm a master in staying in the here and now." You do it to enrich your life with inner peace and calmness no other mean could provide.

What we practice is going to become habit.

Intentionally adopting good habits can free our lives of many displeasures. What do I mean by habit? An activity that comes naturally to us, without the need to think about it. It's intuition, it's second nature. While this may be good news for us when we decide to adopt good habits, the following sentences are also true in case of our already existing – maybe bad – habits.

In order to be able to change our lives and practice into the right direction, first we need to get aware of our bad habits. We need to recognize them and stop doing them once we identify them. Otherwise the laws of practice will apply to them and we don't want to enforce bad habits.

Secondly, we need to be aware of what we want to achieve; have a plan of actions which we intentionally repeat to reach our goal. Repeating something intentionally, practicing it over a period of time will create a habit. This knowledge can grant us some comfort, peace of mind. If we stick to the process of practicing, our habit goal will be achieved. We don't need to stress over the results. We just need to repeat whatever action we know will take us to the desired outcome. Once you successfully achieve something by persistent practice, you'll get an empirical proof that relentless practice pays off. You get in control of your life.

It's all up to you; if you choose to invest time and energy in practice, some weeks will pass and you'll become more accomplished in something, you'll adopt a new habit, you'll conquer a new height. If you choose to do nothing and not practice, those weeks will pass anyway.

Don't look for shortcuts.

Cheating discipline doesn't work, neither on short nor on long-term. There are no hacks you can apply here. As Jim Rohn said, "You can't hire someone else to do your push-ups for you." Anything in life worth reaching won't give you satisfaction if it comes with little or no effort.

Many people miss or reject this point out of fear of discomfort. Others find the pain of work and effort annoying, unwanted. Some pride themselves as being resourceful if they can find the shortest path. Sure, this skill works for traffic jams, finishing a project and such. But when it comes to adoption of good habits or any other self-improvement-related subjects, shortcuts are self-sabotage.

People also tend to focus on the outcome, on the final goal, the "thing" they want to get out of the effort they make. Sadly, the very outcome gives the smallest satisfaction in the entire process. Just think about it. Recall something for which you worked a long time and succeeded. Was the catharsis really the end? Or did you feel more satisfaction after finishing all you needed to do on a random day against all the odds? Weren't you happier when your newly learned skills proved to be useful in an everyday task? Life is really the road, not the destination.

Make your desire to fully experience the work, the road. Stay focused and know that you're on the good track when you practice what you need. No goal will seem too big, too overwhelming, if you learn to find satisfaction in the process because then, as long as you're in the process, each day will have something satisfactory. Have small chunks of milestones for every day that you can complete with a reasonable amount of focus and effort. Carry on.

Slowly but steadily you can achieve whatever you want. I know that the concept of slow is not valued today. When we talk about self-improvement – things like adopting new habits, learning to discipline the mind – things take time. Don't rush yourself, don't be impatient. Don't create unrealistic expectations for yourself. Be objectively aware of what and how quickly you can do.

How to be objectively aware? By distancing yourself from your thoughts; separate yourself from them. Remember the observing mind? The more connected you become with it, the less you'll judge yourself. Just quietly observe your thoughts, don't label them, don't identify with them.

Make a habit of using your observing mind daily. Practice it through meditation. It will help you become more self-aware. Sit down, close your eyes, take a few deep breaths, and whenever a thought or emotion comes into your mind, notice it with gentle compassion. Then let it go.

Increased self-awareness helps you make better decisions regarding what's a reasonable goal to aim for. Having reasonable goals will keep you anxiety-free so you'll be able to focus on the process.

Key takeaways to discipline your mind:

- Practice is not simply for artistic and athletic endeavors. Everything worth achieving in life takes practice.

- The best practice occurs when you are present in the moment and completely focused on the task at hand. When our mind is disciplined, we are willing to delay gratification to work toward achieving something truly meaningful, rather than getting sidetracked by the distraction of instant gratification that will offer little value to our lives in the long-term.

- We can intentionally create the habits we want in our lives by being aware of the goal we want to achieve, breaking it down into steps that will require our repetitive practice and focus, and performing those steps repeatedly without judgment, until they become second nature to us.

Closing Thoughts

Disciplining the mind is not something that comes easily or naturally to us. Our minds are chatty, buzzing, and active all the time. Even advanced meditators can't shut their minds off completely. They are just good at letting go of the thoughts and jumping back to the present moment. Making attempts to make our minds a bit more disciplined, however, pays off even if we can't do it perfectly.

Here are a few of the benefits that come from having a disciplined mind:

- You become keenly aware of the things that are within and beyond your control. You accept responsibility for where you are in your life and your response to what happens to you. You do not waste precious time trying to place blame, or wait for someone else to rescue you and improve your life for you. You understand that meaningful and lasting change comes from within.

- You approach your life with your eyes wide open. You recognize that everything in life is a tradeoff and that when you choose to pursue one goal or focus on one area of your life, there will be a cost in that you are unable to devote your time and energy to other areas. You understand that it is possible to have it all – just not all at the same time. You set your priorities and maintain your focus on achieving your goals.

- You recognize that stress and negative emotions are not something you can avoid or banish from your life. They are inevitable and everyone experiences them. But you understand that you have the power to control the way you respond to them. You know that stress and negative feelings are really a manifestation of needs that aren't being met and you are willing to put in the time and effort to discover what those unmet needs are and find a healthy way to address them.

- You work to overcome temptations and are able to forego instant gratification in favor of more meaningful and valuable delayed gratification. You keep your eye on the prize and maintain your focus and effort in trying to reach your long-term goals without getting distracted and allowing your progress to get derailed.

- You accept that you are a work in progress. You know you will make mistakes and fail at times in your life, but you don't let it get you down and you aren't too hard on yourself because you know it's all a part of the learning and growing process we call life.

In order to have a more disciplined mind, try to keep the following tips in mind:

- Try not to spend too much time worrying about what others think of you. They are too busy worrying about their own problems and challenges to judge you as much as you think they are. Remember that your identity and feeling of self-worth should come from within, not from the opinions of others.

- Always be willing to challenge and re-evaluate your beliefs to make sure that they still fit you today. Speak to people with differing viewpoints and do some research to make sure that they aren't negative and outdated. If you are presented with facts or evidence that warrants it, be willing to adapt or discard them instead of just clinging to them because they are comforting.

- Approach social media in moderation. Be self-aware and know when you are taking the opinions of others too much to heart. Be willing to step away when it is taking up too much of your time and energy or negatively affecting your self-confidence.

- Find your passion and purpose in life and pursue it with abandon.

- Don't be afraid to fail. Failure is a necessary part of life because it teaches us some of the best lessons and enables us to grow. Accept it and learn from it as you continuously try to improve yourself.

- Live in the present. Focus your mind and practice, practice, practice. Everything worth achieving in life requires it.

Thank you for choosing this book to read and for making me a small part of your self-improvement journey on your quest to develop a more disciplined mind. I wish for you a chance to live your best life. Start moving today in the direction of your dreams knowing that you are now equipped with some additional strategies, as well as the power within you to create the life you want for yourself. Accept responsibility for your own happiness and start taking action right away.

I believe in you!

Zoe

Reference

Boyd, John. Zimbardo, Philip. *The Time Paradox: Using the New Psychology of Time to Your Advantage*. Atria Books. 2008.

Cicchetti, D., Walker, E. Editorial: Stress and development: Biological and psychological consequences. Development and Psychopathology, 13(3), 413-418. 2001.

Crowther, Bosley. Walt Disney. Encyclopedia Britannica. 2018. https://www.britannica.com/biography/Walt-Disney

Goleman, Daniel. *Emotional Intelligence*. London: Bloomsbury. 2010

Harvard Health Publishing. Understanding the stress response. Harvard Health Publishing. 2018. https://www.health.harvard.edu/staying-healthy/understanding-the-stress-response

Liden, Matt. 8 Buddhist Tips For Dealing With Anger. Study Buddhism. 2018. https://studybuddhism.com/en/essentials/how-to/8-buddhist-tips-for-dealing-with-anger

Manson, Mark. No, You Can't Have It All. Mark Manson. 2014. https://markmanson.net/you-cant-have-it-all

Manson, Mark. *The subtle art of not giving a f*ck.* Strawberry Hills, NSW: ReadHowYouWant, 2017.

Maslow, A. H. (1943). A theory of human motivation. Psychological Review, 50(4), 370-396. http://dx.doi.org/10.1037/h0054346

Mehrabian, Albert. Albert Mehrabian Communication Studies. IOJT. 2013. http://www.iojt-dc2013.org/~/media/Microsites/Files/IOJT/110 42013-Albert-Mehrabian-Communication-Studies.ashx

Pease, Allan. Pease, Barbara. *The Definitive Book of Body Language: The Hidden Meaning Behind People's Gestures and Expressions.* Bantam. 2006.

Pressfield, Steven. The Art of War. Black Irish Entertainment LLC. 2002.

Robinson, Lawrence. Smith, Melinda. Segal, Robert. Stress Management. Helpfulguide. 2018. https://www.helpguide.org/articles/stress/stress-management.htm

Rook, K. S. (1984). The negative side of social interaction: Impact on psychological well-being. Journal of Personality and Social Psychology, 46(5), 1097-1108. http://dx.doi.org/10.1037/0022-3514.46.5.1097

Rosenberg, Marshall B. PhD. Nonviolent Communication. PuddleDancer Press; Third Edition. 2015.

Squier, Chemmie. Why Do We Get So Obsessed With 'Likes' On Social Media? Grazia Daily. 2016. https://graziadaily.co.uk/life/opinion/care-likes-social-media/

Schwarzenegger, Arnold. Total Recall. Simon&Schuster. 2013.

Thoits, Peggy A. "Stress, Coping, and Social Support Processes: Where Are We? What Next?" Journal of Health and Social Behavior,

1995,   53-79.

http://www.jstor.org/stable/2626957

Sterner, Thomas M. The Practicing Mind. New
World Library. 2012.

Endnotes

[i] Manson, Mark. No, You Can't Have It All. Mark Manson. 2014.
https://markmanson.net/you-cant-have-it-all

[ii] Manson, Mark. No, You Can't Have It All. Mark Manson. 2014.
https://markmanson.net/you-cant-have-it-all

[iii] Boyd, John. Zimbardo, Philip. *The Time Paradox: Using the New Psychology of Time to Your Advantage*. Atria Books. 2008.

[iv] Mehrabian, Albert. Albert Mehrabian Communication Studies. IOJT. 2013.
http://www.iojt-dc2013.org/~/media/Microsites/Files/IOJT/11042013-Albert-Mehrabian-Communication-Studies.ashx

[v] Pease, Allan. Pease, Barbara. *The Definitive Book of Body Language: The Hidden Meaning Behind People's Gestures and Expressions*. Bantam. 2006.

[vi] Pease, Allan. Pease, Barbara. *The Definitive Book of Body Language: The Hidden Meaning Behind People's Gestures and Expressions*. Bantam. 2006.

[vii] Pease, Allan. Pease, Barbara. *The Definitive Book of Body Language: The Hidden Meaning Behind People's Gestures and Expressions.* Bantam. 2006.

[viii] Harvard Health Publishing. Understanding the stress response. Harvard Health Publishing. 2018.
https://www.health.harvard.edu/staying-healthy/understanding-the-stress-response

[ix] Robinson, Lawrence. Smith, Melinda. Segal, Robert. Stress Management. Helpfulguide. 2018.
https://www.helpguide.org/articles/stress/stress-management.htm

[x] Thoits, Peggy A. "Stress, Coping, and Social Support Processes: Where Are We? What Next?" Journal of Health and Social Behavior, 1995, 53-79.
http://www.jstor.org/stable/2626957

[xi] Rook, K. S. (1984). The negative side of social interaction: Impact on psychological well-being. Journal of Personality and Social Psychology, 46(5), 1097-1108.
http://dx.doi.org/10.1037/0022-3514.46.5.1097

[xii] Squier, Chemmie. Why Do We Get So Obsessed With 'Likes' On Social Media? Grazia Daily. 2016.
https://graziadaily.co.uk/life/opinion/care-likes-social-media/

[xiii] Pressfield, Steven. The Art of War. Black Irish Entertainment LLC. 2002.

[xiv] Pressfield, Steven. The Art of War. Black Irish Entertainment LLC. 2002.

[xv] Pressfield, Steven. The Art of War. Black Irish Entertainment LLC. 2002.

[xvi] Pressfield, Steven. The Art of War. Black Irish Entertainment LLC. 2002.

[xvii] Liden, Matt. 8 Buddhist Tips For Dealing With Anger. Study Buddhism. 2018. https://studybuddhism.com/en/essentials/how-to/8-buddhist-tips-for-dealing-with-anger

[xviii] Rosenberg, Marshall B. PhD. Nonviolent Communication. PuddleDancer Press; Third Edition. 2015.

[xix] Maslow, A. H. (1943). A theory of human motivation. Psychological Review, 50(4), 370-396. http://dx.doi.org/10.1037/h0054346

[xx] Crowther, Bosley. Walt Disney. Encyclopedia Britannica. 2018. https://www.britannica.com/biography/Walt-Disney

[xxi] Sterner, Thomas M. The Practicing Mind. New World Library. 2012.

[xxii] Sterner, Thomas M. The Practicing Mind. New World Library. 2012.

[xxiii] Schwarzenegger, Arnold. Total Recall. Simon&Schuster. 2013.

92758426R00120

Made in the USA
Middletown, DE
10 October 2018